D1094247

Twayne's English Authors Series

Thomas Deloney

TEAS 323

Part of the Good Shepherd stained glass window in the St. Nicholas Church in Newbury, England. The window commemorates the famous clothier John Winchcombe, Deloney's Jack of Newbury, whose generosity helped to construct the building.

THOMAS DELONEY

By EUGENE P. WRIGHT

North Texas State University

TWAYNE PUBLISHERS
A DIVISION OF G. K. HALL & CO., BOSTON

Published in 1981 by Twayne Publishers,
A Division of G. K. Hall & Co.

Printed on permanent/durable acid-free paper and bound
in the United States of America

First Printing

Library of Congress Cataloging in Publication Data

Wright, Eugene Patrick, 1936–
Thomas Deloney.

(Twayne's English authors series ; TEAS 323)
Bibliography: p. 141–45
Includes index.
1. Deloney, Thomas, 1543?–1600—Criticism and interpretation.
PR2244.D2Z95   1981   823'.3   81-272
ISBN 0-8057-6761-4   AACR1

For L. W. W.

Contents

About the Author

Eugene P. Wright took the Ph.D. in English Literature at the University of Texas at Austin in 1966. His book *The Joanna Southcott Collection* (1969) was later reprinted in *Texas Quarterly*. He has also published articles in the *South-Central Bulletin, McNeese Review, English in Texas*, and others. Postgraduate studies in English Renaissance literature have taken him to London, Newbury, Reading, and Colnbrook, England, and to Washington, D.C.

Professor Wright teaches English at North Texas State University, Denton, where he specializes in English Renaissance literature.

Preface

Thomas Deloney, Elizabethan silk weaver and writer, is known to most
students of literature only as the author of *The Gentle Craft*, a prose
work Thomas Dekker used as his source for *The Shoemakers' Holiday*.
Some few others know him as one of a group of Elizabethan writers
including George Gascoigne, John Lyly, Sir Philip Sidney, Robert
Greene, Thomas Lodge, and Thomas Nashe who experimented with
prose fiction before there was anything generally called a novel. Only
scholars who specialize in the English Renaissance will have read his
ballads and novels; and as a result, few readers are aware of Deloney's
considerable talents as a literary craftsman, his contemporary popularity, and his role of innovator in the genre of prose fiction.

One reason Deloney is little known to most students of literature is
that his works were literally read out of existence. Many of his ballads
that were printed as broadsides have doubtless disappeared because of
the impermanence of single sheets. None of his four novels is extant in
original editions. Until Francis O. Mann collected the known works
into one edition in the early twentieth century, the ballads and novels
existed only in single editions and, in some cases, unique copies found
in the British Library or elsewhere. But Mann's *The Works of Thomas
Deloney* (1912) and Merritt Lawlis's *The Novels of Thomas Deloney*
(1961) placed copies of Deloney's works in the hands of readers in collected form for the first time since the sixteenth and early seventeenth
centuries, when all of the works were in print or generally available at
the same time. Since the appearance of Mann's collection, scholars in
growing numbers have paid attention to Deloney. Instead of being
considered an historical embodiment of Shakespeare's balladmonger
Autolycus or a curious silk weaver who wrote some prose romances to
augment his income, modern scholars of English literature now recognize Deloney as a middle-class Englishman who had a good education, spent a period of apprenticeship writing ballads, and finally wrote
four significant prose works which altered the course of English prose
fiction.

In the present study I have attempted to pull together the few pieces
of evidence concerning the life of Deloney, to fill in the gaps with what
is known about the social, political, economic, and religious life of the

middle-class Elizabethan, and to formulate as complete a picture of Thomas Deloney as the facts and reasonable extrapolation will allow. Secondly, I have attempted to look critically at the major poems and the novels in order to arrive at a clear understanding of what Deloney was trying to do and to judge how well he succeeded in achieving his purposes. Finally, I have tried to review Deloney's early and modern reputations and, most important, to discuss his place in the history of English prose fiction. Because I am dealing with a writer about whom relatively little is known and with a canon that is both partial and probably somewhat corrupt (since there exist few first editions of the poems and none of the prose works), my conjectures about Deloney and his works must be liable to further discoveries. The fortunate discovery of a first edition of one or more of the prose works or the chance finding of a significant reference to Deloney in the public records of some small clothing town would be very useful in bringing sharper focus to the picture.

This book was written over a three-year period in such diverse places as Texas, Colorado, and England. I am grateful for awards from the North Texas State University Faculty Research Committee, from Professor Sam Henderson, Chairman of the NTSU English Department, and from Dean Jim Pearson of the NTSU College of Arts and Sciences. I also thank Professors David B. Kesterson and James T. F. Tanner, Chairmen of the Schedule Committee. The staffs of the British Library; the public library at Newbury, Berkshire, England; the Southern Methodist University library; and the NTSU library were patient and helpful, and I thank them. I am grateful also to Mrs. Peg Antonatos, NTSU English Department Administrative Assistant, for seeing that I had whatever materials I needed for my work and to Sandra Gilbert and Sherryl Taylor for helping to type the manuscript.

I owe a special thanks to Professors Jim Linebarger and A. J. Koinm for reading the manuscript and making many valuable suggestions. Their help was, as always, professional and expert. I am indebted to TEAS field editor Arthur F. Kinney for his scholarly advice relevant to the Renaissance generally and Deloney specifically. His careful work on the manuscript improved the quality both of the ideas and the craftsmanship. One of the joys of doing scholarly work is having friends and colleagues take an interest in the material. Professors L. Robert Stevens, J. F. Kobler, Giles Mitchell, Howard L. Ford, Richard B. Sale, and Marsue Johnson offered almost daily help and encouragement during the project. Thanks also to my graduate students who read Deloney at my urging and taught me much about his works: Shelly Angel, Ollie Adamson, Joe Clarke, Phyllis Eccleston, Betty Groves, D'Ann Madewell, Jessie Stevens. And to Wanda, who makes it all worthwhile.

EUGENE P. WRIGHT

Denton, Texas

Chronology

1543? Born, probably in Norwich, England.

1583 Publishes translations of two Latin pieces, "A Declaration made by the Archbishop of Collen" and "The Proclamation and Edict of the Archbyshop."

1586 Publishes "The Lamentation of Beccles" and "The Death and Execution of Fourteen Most Wicked Traitors." October, his son Richard is baptized at St. Giles Church, Cripplegate. December, the infant Richard dies.

1588 March 23, "A Pleasant Dialogue Between Truth, and Blind Ignorance" and "The Overthrow of Proud Holofornes" entered in the Stationers' Register. August 10, "The Queenes Visiting of the Campe at Tilsburie" and "The Happie Obtaining of the Great Galleazzo" entered in the Stationers' Register. August 31, "The Straunge and Most Cruell Whippes" entered in the Stationers' Register.

1591 August 26, "A Maidens Choice Twixt Age and Youth" entered in the Stationers' Register.

1592 Robert Greene condemns Deloney's works as "triviall trinkets and threedbare trash."

1593 Publishes *Garland of Good Will*. Gabriel Harvey classifies Deloney as one of "the common Pamfleteers of London." Thomas Nashe calls upon Deloney to defend the reputation of the balladmonger William Elderton. June 16, "The Lamentation of Shores Wife" entered in the Stationers' Register. June 27, "A Gentlewomans Complaint" entered in the Stationers' Register.

1594 March 22, "A Most Sweet Song of an English Merchant" entered in the Stationers' Register.

1595 Sent to jail for distributing a printed complaint against foreign weavers.

1596 Publishes "Ballad on the Want of Corn" (not extant), for which he is sought by the law for having published "foolish and disorderly matter."

1597 March 7, *Jack of Newbury* entered in Stationers' Register. July 8, a ballad, "The first parte of Iacke of Newberye," entered in the Stationers' Register. October 19, *The Gentle Craft* entered in the Stationers' Register. Probably published *Thomas of Reading* during the summer months.

1598   Probably published *The Gentle Craft, Part 2*. January 5, *Canaans Calamitie* entered in the Stationers' Register.

1600   "Died poorly . . . and was honestly buried."

CHAPTER 1

"The Balletting Silke Weaver"

SPEAKING of the middle–class Englishman of the Elizabethan period, Louis B. Wright raises the question of the worth of middle-class values and ideas: "Why resurrect dead dullness? Is the taste of the average citizen of the present time not deplorable enough without unearthing the crudities of his ancestors?"[1] The answer in some cases is "yes." But that is not to say that all middle-class authors are either dead or dull. Some, like Thomas Deloney, while being spokesmen for and to the Elizabethan middle class, were witty, careful craftsmen.

Deloney's most significant contributions to English literature are his four novels, but he also wrote many broadsides and poems. In 1583 he translated into English a proclamation and letter in Latin by Archbishop Gebhardt of Collen and a reply to Gebhardt by Pope Gregory XIII dealing with Gebhardt's decision to marry. A "T. D." (probably Thomas Deloney)[2] translated parts of a book by Bonaventure Des Périers (1500?–1544) entitled *Les Contes ou les nouvelles recreations et joyeux devis*, which in the translation became *The Mirrour of Mirth and pleasant Conceits*.[3]

Contemporary references to Deloney and the fact that his novels were published as chapbooks well into the eighteenth century indicate his popularity as a writer. So completely were his novels read that no first-edition copy of any of them is extant. During the sixteenth and seventeenth centuries he was well known to his contemporaries, some of whom were writers influenced by his stories, style, and realism. Yet less is known about the life of Thomas Deloney than any other significant writer of the period: he has remained obscure, partly because he was a member of the merchant class, about whom contemporary historians wrote little. Deloney, like his character Jack of Newbury, chose to stay within the merchant class rather than seek to rise by patronage and favor and so is, perhaps, directly responsible for the paucity of records. The genre Deloney chose to work in also contributed to his obscurity. Street ballads were treated contemptuously by critics familiar with the poetic efforts of Edmund Spenser, Philip Sidney, or Chris-

15

topher Marlowe. Prose fiction was also a medium little recognized in a period when dramatic literature was at its greatest. And, of course, Deloney's religious translations were matters of passing concern, and that only to a few.

No documents have yet been uncovered that will explain who Deloney's parents were, how extensive his formal education was, whom he married, or how many children he fathered. There remains for us neither a portrait of Deloney nor a description of his physical appearance. What is known of Deloney is gleaned from scanty entries in the Stationers' Register, from remarks made about him by his contemporaries, and, especially, from his works. With the broad outline of the puzzle of Deloney's life thus sketched, the missing parts must be supplied by inference or speculation based upon a general knowledge of middle-class life in Elizabethan England.

Deloney's death date can be set at 1600 with some certainty, for Will Kemp, the famous comic actor, reported that year that Deloney had recently "dyed poorely . . . and was honestly buried."[4] But the date of his birth is a matter of considerable speculation. J. W. Ebbsworth, contributor to the DNB on Deloney, lists 1543 as Deloney's birthdate,[5] and several later dictionaries and encyclopedias have accepted the suggestion. But in fact there is no evidence to establish a date of birth. Merritt Lawlis suggests that 1560 would be "a better guess" at a birthdate, but he admits that he has no evidence;[6] his opinion rests on the assumption that Deloney's earliest extant ballads (published in 1586) were the work of a man younger than forty-three. "It is impossible," states Francis O. Mann, "to give even a rough guess at the date of his birth."[7]

The place of Deloney's birth is also a matter of speculation. Mann strongly suggests that Deloney was born in Norwich, but part of his evidence comes from a misreading of Thomas Nashe.[8] Nevertheless, Deloney's earliest broadside ballad, "The Lamentation of Beccles," was published in Norwich. In addition, his name is probably of French ancestry,[9] and many of his writings show an anti-Catholic bias. Both of these facts also suggest that Deloney lived in Norwich, for many of the Flemish and Huguenot Protestants who fled their homelands to escape religious persecution during the fifteenth and sixteenth centuries settled in Norfolk. Moreover, many of these refugees, like Deloney, were clothiers; John Strype reports that "Among the trading Strangers that came over into England from Flanders and those Parts for their Religion, in the said Queen Elizabeth's Reign, there were divers of this Sort that dealt in dressing and preparing Silk for the other trades."[10]

Although Deloney's first known literary venture, *A Declaration made by the Archbishop of Collen upon the Deede of his Mariage* (1583), was published in London, there is a great deal of evidence to tie Deloney to Norwich in the early part of his life. "The Balletting Silke Weaver of Norwich," while not an accurate quotation, is probably true.

Wherever he might have spent his childhood, Deloney's ability to use English clearly and effectively, his knowledge of Latin and French, his borrowings from contemporaneous literature, and his allusions to history and classical literature all suggest that he had at least a good grammar-school education. Louis Wright discusses the English school system during the time of Deloney which, he says, was well developed and available to students of all classes.[11] Much of the "bohemian world of literature," says Wright, "was peopled by bright young men of humble parentage, who had received their background of learning in the free schools of the land."[12] Deloney, certainly, was one of these bright young men.

It is clear that the early part of Deloney's adult life was spent as a silk weaver, for several contemporaries refer to him as one. And, of course, many of his works show him to be a willing, and perhaps even a hired, spokesman for the clothiers of England. The next extant reference to Deloney, however, comes three years later in 1586, when the broadside ballad "The Lamentation of Beccles" was published. In that same year two brief entries in the parish register of St. Giles, Cripplegate, suggest that Deloney was married and living in London. The first entry, dated October 1586, records the christening of a son: "Richard Delonie sonne of Thomas Delonie silk-weaver the. 16."[13] Two months later there appears a sadder entry under "Burials in December 1586" which reads, "Richard Delonie sonne of John Delonie silkweaver the. 21."[14] "John" may be a clerical error for "Thomas," for, as Mann points out, the references in the church register almost certainly apply to Deloney the writer. Three years after he had begun to publish his writings, he was still known as "Thomas Delonie, silk-weaver."

During the next six years Deloney turned out a large number of ballads, enough so that at the death of the famous ballad writer William Elderton, Deloney appears to have inherited his title as king of the ballad writers. When Gabriel Harvey attacked the literary quality of Elderton's ballads, Thomas Nashe called upon several obviously well-known ballad writers, including Deloney, to rise to the defense of their fellow:

Hough Thomas Delone, Phillip Stubs, Robert Armin, & C. Your father *Elderton* is abus'd. Reuenge on course paper and want of matter, that hath most
sacriligiously contaminated the diuine spirit & quintessence of a penny a
quart.[15]

In answer, Harvey, suggesting that Nashe should write of more significant matters, advised him to "boast lesse with Thomas Delone, or to
atchieve more with Thomas More."[16] Robert Greene, himself reduced
to pamphleteering in order to earn a living, also condemned Deloney's
ballads as worthless:

Such triviall trinkets and threedbare trash, had better seemed T. D. whose
braines beaten to the yarking up of Ballades, might more lawfully have
glaunst at the quaint conceits of conny-catching and Crosse-biting.[17]

But Greene was also using this occasion to promote his own work.

Thomas Deloney was, therefore, if not praised by the University
Wits, at least well known as a writer by the early 1590s. Acting much
like an early-day journalist, Deloney wrote ballads on newsworthy
items. Sometimes his opinions about such events led to legal action. In
1595 Deloney was arrested for distributing offensive material, a complaint to the authorities against foreign weavers who came to England
to practice their trade without following the rules of the Weaver's
Company. Charging unfair trade practices, Deloney and fourteen
other English weavers drafted a complaint and sent printed copies to
pastors of several French and Dutch churches in London, hoping that
the pastors would demand that their refugee parishioners obey the
rules. The refugee problem, when added to the problems of unemployment, famine, and inflation, was surely a matter of survival for
many of Deloney's company. Deloney's complaint and his request that
established business practices be followed are understandable, but
instead of righting what Deloney and the others saw as an unjust situation, the pastors had the signers of the complaint sent to jail. Deloney
gained his release only by petitioning the Lord Chief Justice.[18] Strype
reports that in 1596 the Lord Mayor of London was looking for Deloney to arrest him for writing a "scurrilous Ballad" entitled "Ballad on
the Want of Corn," but could not find him.[19] The offensive ballad was
ordered burned and no copy is extant. It is clear from these references
that during the last two decades of the sixteenth century Thomas
Deloney became a political spokesman for his class, as well as an enter-

tainer; sometimes the roles coincided, earning for him at the same time the devotion of the middle class and the enmity of government officials.

Perhaps Deloney's problems with the authorities caused him to shun public notice for the last few years of his life. He may have continued to write ballads, for Will Kemp in 1600 referred to him as "the great ballad maker, T. D., alias Thomas Deloney,"[20] but, of greater importance, in the last four years of his life Deloney published four novels. Only two of his novels are listed in the Stationers' Register, *Jack of Newbury* on 7 March 1597 and *The Gentle Craft* on 19 October 1597. Although no conclusive evidence exists to date the other two, it is likely that *Thomas of Reading* was the second novel published, coming sometime during the summer of 1597. The final work, *The Gentle Craft, Part 2*, was probably published early in 1598.

Like so many events of his life, the details of Deloney's death are shrouded in mystery. Will Kemp tells us that he "died poorly," as John Lyly and Robert Greene did. But in Kemp's criticism of balladmakers as a class, he remained tender toward Deloney, whom he called the "late general" of the balladmakers. Kemp does not use the event of Deloney's death to delcare how God's justice has fallen upon a chief offender. Instead, he reports only that Deloney "was honestly buried."[21]

CHAPTER 2

The Poetry

I Deloney and the Ballad Tradition

THOMAS Deloney's modern literary reputation rests primarily
upon his four novels, all written during the last three years of his
life; but to evaluate his achievement we must also understand why to
his contemporaries his fame was as a ballad writer. The tradition of the
popular ballad, a literary form Deloney used freely, had its origin in
the obscurity of the Middle Ages. The beginnings of the general tradition or of a specific ballad are unknown, for the early ballad belongs
to folk culture, and although in its original form it probably was written and sung by a single composer, it became the property of the people who changed it and incorporated it into their lives. Because of the
popularity of ballads, minstrels were able to earn a living by wandering
from town to town singing the old ballad stories of Lord Randal, Sir
Patrick Spens, and hard-hearted Barbara Allen.

Minstrels, however, mark a second phase in the history of ballads.
They had no part in the development of the folk ballads in the purest
sense, for folk ballads were the traditional songs of the people and were
used for their own entertainment; minstrels were professional enter-
tainers who were usually attached to some nobleman or were available
for hire to sing at taverns or on street corners. While these minstrels
sang the traditional ballads, they also often wrote their own, and these
were more likely to represent the political or personal views of the
singer. Distinctions between the types of ballads began to blur when,
after the introduction of the printing press into England near the end
of the fifteenth century, ballads of all types began to be printed on
single sheets (or broadsides) about the size of a handbill, and were sold
for a penny or less to the public. Such ballads fell generally into two
categories: the literary ballad and the street ballad.[1] Deloney wrote
both types.

The folk ballad, the literary ballad, and the street ballad have certain
characteristics in common. Ballads are narrative verses of a dramatic

historical, romantic, or tragic episode. Character development is slight, scenes change rapidly, and the point of view changes from narrative to dialogue only when the story requires heightened pathos or detail. As with characterization, language seldom detracts from the essential movement of the story being told. Imagery is of the simplest sort; rarely in ballads are there the extended conceits one finds in the lyrical poems of Petrarch and his followers. Knights are described merely as "good" (like Sir Patrick Spens) or "gallant"; lovers are "true"; beds are "soft and narrow" (as in "Lord Randal"); and ladies are "fair." The story is never diluted by complex philosophy, characterization, or imagery.

Other characteristics of ballads are repetition and parallelism, used to help the singer remember the essential facts of the ballad or to allow the listener another opportunity to catch a vital detail he might have missed. In "Sir Patrick Spens," for example, the pathos in the poem is achieved by repeatedly picturing the wives of the drowned sailors waiting for their men to return from the sea, although this repetition is more than just mnemonic. Here repetition emphasizes an especially important part of the story.

> O lang, lang may their ladies sit,
>   Wi thair fans into their hand,
> Or eir they se Sir Patrick Spens
>   Cum sailing to the land.
>
> O lang, lang may the ladies stand,
>   Wi thair gold kems in their hair,
> Waiting for thair ain deir lords,
>   For they'll se thame na mair.

"Sir Patrick Spens" also illustrates the meter of ballads. All English ballads are strophic; the meter is almost always iambic, although metrical variation, usually in the form of anapestic substitutions, is regularly employed. The stanzas are characteristically either two rhymed lines of iambic tetrameter or four lines alternating iambic tetrameter and iambic trimeter, with the second and fourth lines rhyming.

Deloney uses both types, as well as several other stanzaic forms not usually found in folk ballads. In "The Lamentable Death of King Iohn," for example, Deloney uses a four-line stanza which is a modification of the two-line, four-beat stanza of the folk ballad. Deloney's lines are couplets containing five beats to each line, as the musical notation accompanying the 1602 printing of the poem shows; the main difference between this stanzaic form and that of some folk ballads is that Deloney's tune is repeated every four lines, whereas that of the folk ballad usually is repeated every two lines. But the basic relationship of Deloney's poem to the traditional two-line stanzas with four beats a line is obvious:

> A Trecherous deede forthwith I shall you tell,
> Which on King *Iohn* vpon a sudden fell;
> To Lincolneshire proceeding on his way,
> At *Swinestead* Abby, one whole night he lay.
>   (SH, p. 399; sig. B4)[2]

Most of his ballads, however, follow the second traditional form. Deloney's "The Death and Execution of 14 Most Wicked Traitors" is an example of his use of the four-line stanza, alternating tetrameter and trimeter:

> Reioyce in hart, good people all
>   sing praise to God on hye,
> Which hath preserved vs by his power
>   from traitors tiranny.
>   (MB, p. 464)

Few critics through the years have placed much value on the street ballad; most have considered it a cheap imitation of the vigorous folk ballads of the Middle Ages. As I have shown, the "balladmongers" were ridiculed by educated men during Deloney's lifetime, while the Puritan attack upon poetry during the sixteenth century almost certainly was aimed to a large extent at the street ballads littering London and other English towns. Roger Ascham, tutor to young Elizabeth, complained in 1570 that "shoppes in London should not be so full of lewd and rude rymes, as commonlie they are. But not the ripest of tong be readiest to write: And many dayly in setting out bookes and balettes make great shew of blossomes and buddes, in whom is neither roote of learning nor frute of wisedome at all."[3] Even Thomas Lodge, who in 1579 defended poetry against the enthusiastic attack of Stephen Gosson, agreed that "foolishe ballets" constituted "an abuse of poetry." Lodge called for "the expullcion of such enormities," and said, "Beleeue mee the magestrates may take aduise (as I know wisely can) to roote out those odd rymes which runnes in euery rascales mouth, sauoring of rybaldry."[4] But perhaps the most vehement in his denunciation of the balladmongers was the more generally agreeable William Webbe. After praising such poets as Chaucer, Lydgate, Spenser, and other masters of English poetry,[5] he condemns the "barbarous immitatours" of good poets:

If I let passe the vncountable rabble of ryming Ballet makers and compylers of sencelesse sonnets, who be most busy to stuffe euery stall full of grosse deuises and vnlearned Pamphlets, I trust I shall with the best sort be held excused. For though many such can frame an Ale-house song of fiue or sixe score verses, hobbling vppon some tune of a Northern iygge, or Robyn hoode, or La lubber, etc. and perhappes obserue iust number of sillables, eyght in one line, sixe in an other, and there withall an A to make a iercke in the ende [a probable reference to nonsense syllables sometimes added as a stylistic device[6]]: yet if these might be accounted Poets (as it is sayde some of them make meanes to be promoted to the Lawrell) surely we shall shortly haue whole swarmes of Poets: and euery one that can frame a Booke in Ryme, though for want of matter it be but in commendations of Copper noses or Bottle Ale, wyll catch at the Garlande due to Poets; whose potticall, poeticall (I should say), heades I would wyshe at their worshipfull comencements might in steede of Lawrell be gorgiously garnished with fayre greene Barley, in token of their good affection to our English Malt.[7]

Modern critics have been no kinder to the Renaissance balladmongers: "As poetry the broadsides," Albert Friedman says, "to be frank, are trash."[8] Most of the street ballads, unlike folk ballads, were written as commercial ventures rather than as deeply felt expressions of admiration, pathos, or wonder. Most were designed to attract the attention of the semiliterate populations of urban communities and therefore often treated subjects in a highly sensational or sentimental manner, much like the tabloid journalism of our own age. Autolycus, the balladmonger of Shakespeare's *The Winter's Tale*, offers for sale broadside ballads of "how a usuer's wife was brought to bed of twenty money bags at a burden, and how she longed to eat adders' heads and toads carbonadoes" and of "a fish that appeared upon the coast on Wednesday the four-score of April, forty thousand fathoms above water" (IV.iv). The temptation is to think of Autolycus as a fictional exaggeration of balladmongers, but the ballad titles listed in the Stationers' Register show that Shakespeare was merely recording an Elizabethan phenomenon.[9]

How many poems Deloney wrote during his lifetime cannot be known. The broadside publication is by its nature impermanent. Most of Deloney's extant poems were collected into three books, all probably first published during the author's lifetime. Some few are included in his published prose works, and a few others exist as uncollected broadsides. There are contemporary references to eight ballads by Deloney that are neither extant nor identifiable. Sir Stephen Slany mentions "Scarcity of Corn Within the Realm" and "A Book for the Silk Weauers,"[10] both of which are lost. Nashe credits Deloney with having written five ballads: "An epistel of Momus and Zoylus,"[11] "Iigge of Iohn for the King," "The Thunderbolt against Swearers," "Repent, England, Repent," and "The Strange Iudgments of God." Although there are copies of ballads on some of these subjects, none can be definitely credited to Deloney.[12] Eight other ballads are ascribed to Deloney with little or no evidence by various collectors of ballads.[13]

The major collections of Deloney's ballads are *The Garland of Good Will*, entered in the Stationers' Register in 1593, and *Strange Histories*, first publication date unknown. The earliest extant edition of *The Garland of Good Will*, published in 1631, contains twenty-seven ballads, most of which were published originally as broadsides. The 1602 edition of *Strange Histories* contains eleven ballads and a prose dialogue between Lady Oxenbridge and some unidentified "Ladies" on the subject of the peasant's revolt during the reign of Henry VII. Mann believes that the works included in this collection had not been circulated previously, since they are arranged in chronological order to fit into a volume rather than being an amorphous collection of previously printed broadsides as is *The Garland of Good Will*.[14] *Canaans Calamitie* or *The dolefull destruction of faire Ierusalem* is the third major book of poetry by Deloney. Entered in the Stationers' Register in January 1598, the book is not a collection, but a single poem of 1278 lines.

At least nine other ballads by Deloney exist only as broadsides. These uncollected poems are primarily those that deal with journalistic matters, such as "The Queenes visiting of the Campe at Tilsburie," "The Straunge and Most Cruell Whippes," and "The Lamentations of Mr. Page's Wife." How many others Deloney wrote is unknown, but his reputation among his contemporaries as "the great ballad maker" suggests that he wrote many more ballads than we have before us today.

Many of Deloney's ballads show that he was a poet perceptive enough of significant human experiences and a craftsman skillful enough to analyze those experiences. I should not care to argue that in Renaissance street ballads there might not be poems of philosophical and literary importance or that Deloney's reputation as a "distinguished writer,"[15] as Hyder Rollins calls him, might justifiably rest on his poetry. Yet he chose his subjects more carefully than many of the balladmongers, and his magnum poetic opus, *Canaans Calamitie*, is the work of a man who had some literary ambitions beyond the pack of Autolycus. The better ballads give a middle-class view of the political, social, religious, and economic problems of their time.

The subjects of the ballads vary. Among the least significant is a ballad on the great fire that destroyed Beccles, a market town in Suffolk. Another ballad, certainly more significant, recounts the English capture of a Spanish galleon in 1588. At least five more of Deloney's ballads deal with other contemporary events of interest to a public who had no newspapers to inform them. Deloney's historical ballads are drawn from those chronicle histories that appealed to the new Elizabethan chauvinism around the time of the Spanish Armada. Ballads covering important events in the lives of King Edgar, Queen Elinor, King John, Edward II, and of Wat Tyler and Jack Straw educated and delighted Deloney's audience. Social questions were considered in such ballads as "The Scarcity of Corn" and "The Lamentation of Mr. Page's Wife." "Virtuous Queen Judith" and "Truth and Ignorance" deal with religious questions, and "Salomon's Good Houswife" and "Repent, England, Repent" treat moral questions. The Elizabethan interest in medieval romance which Deloney was later to exploit in several of his prose episodes begins here, too. "The Death of Rosamond," "Lancelot du Lake," "Patient Grissel," and "The Spanish Lady's Love" are but a few of the romances Deloney served up in the popular medium to an attentive public: the same subjects the dramatists of the time used to appeal to the groundlings were used by Deloney to attract attention to his ballads.

II *Street Ballads*

The street ballad was clearly a marketable product during Deloney's day. No less than forty publishers of ballads are listed in the Stationers' Register before 1580, representing nearly two hundred Elizabethan ballad writers. The subject matter of most street ballads is hardly suited for poetry: deformed pigs, house fires, murders, hangings, monstrous fish, and the like. But the purpose of these poets (if the word "poet" may be used in this context) was primarily commercial. The ballad-mongers were writing on subjects that interested the public, and from that basically economic point of view many of these "poets," Deloney among them, were "successful." Hyder Rollins reports that "Distinguished writers like Deloney, William Elderton, Laurence Price, and Martin Parker may not improbably have received forty shillings for their works."[16] Most of these works, like most of the hasty writings of any age, are insignificant, boring, aesthetically offensive to a mature audience, and therefore are unworthy of scholarly analysis.

But not all of the old street ballads are equally poor. Joseph Ritson believes that Deloney's "Fair Rosamond" is "one of the best of the old English ballads."[17] Francis Gummere admits that among Deloney's extant ballads there is "a piece or so of some literary merit";[18] "The Spanish Lady's Love" is Gummere's favorite. These and other of Deloney's ballads closely resemble the folk ballad in their simplicity and intensity. Just how interested Deloney was in the folk ballad may be deduced from the fact that he includes two traditional ballads in his story of Jack of Newbury; of one of these ballads, "Flodden Field," Deloney insists in his text that "the Commons of *England* made this Song: which to this day is not forgotten of many" (p. 25; sig. E2), and most scholars agree that Deloney composed neither "Flodden Field" nor "Fair Flower of Northumberland," which also appears in *Jack of Newbury*.[19] Perhaps it is his interest in the heroic qualities of the folk ballad that caused Deloney to avoid such topics as "A true relacon of the birth of Three Monsters in the City of Namen in Flounders" and "Tydings of a Huge and Ougly childe born at Arneheim in Gelderland."[20] Deloney is no Autolycus, nor do his ballads play merely upon simple people's base interests in sensationalism or sentimentality; while he for the most part wrote his ballads neither as self-conscious artist nor as historian—his purpose consistently being to write ballads on subjects that would appeal to the people—we would be wrong to dismiss all of his poetic attempts as being "trivial trinkets and threedbare trash." The best of Deloney's ballads possess many of the same qualities that were later to make his prose works successful: a vitality in the telling of an heroic tale, an effective use of dialogue, and a familiar portrayal of the common man.

Deloney loved an heroic story as much as did the scops who sang the praises of the Anglo-Saxon warriors, and Elizabethan England's struggles against the Spanish gave Deloney grist enough for his mill. In "Winning of Cales" (GGW, p. 367; sig. H1), for example, Deloney recounts with such vitality the taking of Cadiz by the Earl of Essex on June 21, 1596, that the ballad rises above the mere hack work of most street ballads. The story begins with the lavishly equipped Spanish moving threateningly against the "valiant and hardy" English:

> Long the proud Spaniard
>   advanced to conquer us,
> Threatening our Country
>   with fire and sword,
> Often preparing
>   their Navy most sumptuous,
> With all the provision
>   that *Spain* could afford.

The vigorous action builds with every stanza as the two great powers clash in naval warfare:

> There might you see the Ships,
>   how they were fired fast:
> And how the men drowned
>   themselves in the Sea,
> There might you hear them cry,
>   wail and weep piteously:
> When as they saw no shift
>   to escape thence away.

When the Spanish are defeated, Deloney lists specifically what happens to the most important of the Spanish ships:

> The great *Saint Philip*,
>   The pride of the Spaniards,
> Was burnt to the bottom
>   and sunk in the sea,
> But the *Saint Andrew*,
>   and eke the *Saint Matthew*,
> We took in fight manly,
>   and brought them away.

Deloney's use of specific detail and his placing the persona on the scene as an observer lends an excitement, an immediacy to the narrative. "We" took the ships, "we" searched the city; the point of view is

that of the common sailor and therefore what Deloney's audience
would have experienced had they been there:[21]

> In some places we did finde
>   pies baking in the Ovens,
> Meat at the fire roasting,
>   and men ran away.

Another ballad concerning the war with Spain also exhibits Deloney's love of an heroic story. "The Happie obtaining of the Great Galleazzo" (MB, p. 468), published in London in 1588, probably shortly
after the battle, is primarily a song of national pride and praise cele-
brating a battle with the Spanish Armada on July 21, 1588. As in many
Elizabethan pamphlets on the subject, Deloney's ballad is largely propaganda. England is "Noble England" and the enemy the "false Spaniards," who come to torture, rape, murder, and pillage the peaceful
English, and of course "to depriue our noble Queene,/both of her life
and crowne." The major reason for English victory is that whereas the
Spanish trusted in force and the Pope, the English trusted in God:

> The Lord no doubt is on our side
>   which soone will worke their fall.

Deloney's love of heroism, however, will not allow God full credit
for the defeat of the satanic Spanish. He plays up the strength of the
enemy ("Great is their number,/of ships vpon the sea"), the magnifi-
cence of their ships ("That like a bulwarke on the sea,/did seeme to
each mans eye"), and the excellence of their equipment ("their proui-
sion wonderfull"). In the face of overpowering superiority, the English
fought "coragiously," capturing one ship and sinking another.

> Like Lions fierce they forward went,
>   to quite this iniurie.
> And bourding them,
>   with strong and mightie hand:
> They kild the men vntill thier Arke,
>   did sinke in Callice sand.

The injury referred to was an attack made upon English longboats
sent to board the galleon of Don Hugo de Moncaldo after the Spanish

had signaled surrender. In this as in other details, Deloney's description closely parallels that of an eyewitness to the battle, the Dutch Emanuel van Meteren, whose objectively written "The miraculous victory atchieved by the English Fleete . . . Upon the Spanish huge Armada" was translated by Richard Hakluyt and printed in his *The Principal Navigations* (1598).

As in news stories of modern days, the poem contains certain specific facts to inform the public. The English had met the superior Spanish fleet at Plymouth. In the ensuing battle the galleon commanded by Don Pedro de Valdez was captured. The ballad then follows the battle across the channel to Calais, where another Spanish ship was damaged and looted by the English. Deloney details such things as the execution of Don Hugo de Moncaldo, commander of the second ship (shot "through his braines"), the foaming sea ("Died and staind like scarlet red"), and the stores captured by the English ("Cannons" and "bread-corne wine and meat").

Strangely, though the purpose of the poem is primarily to rejoice in the capture of Don Pedro's galleon, the details of the capture are vague. We are told that the battle took place at Plymouth, and "There it was taken/vnto our great reliefe." We might assume that, following the tradition of the folk ballads, Deloney understates the main event. His neglect of this sort of historical detail, however, probably had a more immediate political purpose, since the capture of the ship resulted more from Spanish ineptitude than from English valor. Van Meteren reports that when a Spanish ship was set on fire by English cannon, several other Spanish ships, including Don Pedro's galleon, closed to help extinguish the flames. In the operation, heavy seas caused Don Pedro's ship to tangle and break her foremast in another ship's rigging. The ship lay dead in the water, easy prey to Sir Francis Drake.[22] Deloney, probably not finding the details suitable for his purposes, omits them.

The immense amount of extant literature on the Spanish threat and the English victory indicates the importance of the events to the English. Deloney surely had no trouble finding an audience for his journalistic ballads which reported on English victories against the feared enemy. More significant to a modern audience, however, is that the emotions of fear and exhilaration which sparked ancient songs of battle give these ballads a vitality born of justifiable pride in true heroism.

On the other hand, when Deloney strays from writing about actual battles to relating rumors and legends, his ballads become melodramatic. In "Straunge and Most Cruell Whippes" (MB, p. 479) Deloney reports that in July 1588 the English Navy had found cargos of whips aboard two captured Spanish vessels. He assumes that the whips were intended to be used by the Spanish devils against innocent English citizens. Deloney imagines rape, torture, and death being practiced upon English women and children, a picture designed to stir to a froth English anger against the Spanish:

> Although their bodies sweet and fayre
>   their spoyle they ment to make:
> And on them first their filthie lust
>   and pleasure for to take.
> . . . .
> O Ladies fayre what spite were this,
>   your gentle hearts to kill:
> To see these deuilish tyrants thus
>   your childrens bloud to spill.
> What griefe vnto the husband deere,
>   his louing wife to see
> Tormented so before his face
>   with extreme villainie.

What is evident in such ballads as these is chauvinism, not pride. No English children were murdered with the "cruell Whippes," no women raped. (How the alleged discovery of whips aboard Spanish ships conjured in Deloney's imagination the specter of rape is not clear.) Indeed, the discovery of a cargo of whips probably never occurred, for the writer of another ballad of the day reports the same rumor, but decides that it is false:

> Some say two shipps were full of whippes,
> But I thinke they were mistaken.[23]

As Deloney moves farther from events of his day, his ballads lose more of their heroic vigor. Whether or not he was personally a part of the naval force that defeated the powerful Spanish, he was obviously interested in the action, excited by the valor of the English, and proud of his country. When, on the other hand, he tries to strike the same fire from the heroic acts of legendary or historical tales far removed from his own experience, he fails. There is no vitality, for example, in "The

Noble Acts of Arthur of the Round Table, and of Lancelot du Lake"
(GGW, p. 323; sig. C5). In Deloney's narrative, the heroic Lancelot
fought not because his country or his freedom was being attacked; he
simply had nothing else to do:

> When he had rested him a while,
>   to play to game and sport,
> He thought he would go proue himselfe,
>   in some aduenturous sort.

Lancelot's major battle is against the knight Tarquin, who angers
Lancelot by saying, "Both thee and all thy fellowship, I vtterly defie."
Lancelot replies "That's ouermuch," and proceeds to fight and kill his
enemy.

In several of his ballads Deloney succeeds in telling heroic tales without the use of dialogue. Indeed, when he attempts to report the dialogue of some heroes of history or legend, as in the story of Sir Lancelot
du Lake for example, he succeeds only in sounding ridiculous. But
Deloney's ear for dialogue, exhibited most clearly in his novels, can be
seen in several of his more successful ballads. Among the poems published in his three major collections, ten depend heavily upon dialogue.
Three of these are almost entirely in the form of conversation: "Walsingham," "The Spanish Lady's Love," and "A Dialogue betweene
plaine Truth and blind Ignorance."[24]

F. O. Mann points out that Deloney's most successful ballads are
those in which "he has either merely written down or closely imitated
folk tradition"[25] instead of falling into the prosaic habits of the commercial Renaissance balladmongers. "Walsingham" (GGW, p. 365; sig.
G5v), whether its origin is a traditional ballad "merely written down"
or original with Deloney, is successful because it uses the terse dialogue
of folk ballads to present an old man's strong belief in Love (the ever-
fixed mark) and a graceful lament for love (a fickle young woman).
The poem has no long prologue, as many street ballads do, greeting
the audience and preparing it for the story which it is about to hear.
In "Shore's Wife" (GGW, p. 302; sig. A6v), for example, Deloney is
writing for what Mann describes as an audience different from those
for whom folk ballads were an integral part of life. The audience for
street ballads, "passive and not too intelligent,"[26] was greeted, praised,
and given all antecedent action before the writer gets to the heart of
the story. No *in medias res* here:

> Listen, faire Ladies,
> Vnto my misery:
> That liued late in pompous state
>   most delightfully.
> And now by Fortune's faire dissimulation
> Brought to cruell and vncouth plagues,
>   most spightfully.

"Walsingham," however, is delightfully to the point, intense, simple. The poem begins with an old man speaking to a traveler:

> As you came from the holy land
>   of *Walsingham,*
> Met you not with my true loue,
>   by the way as you came?

Deloney successfully dramatizes the old man's unhappiness over losing his beautiful "true loue" by having him talk with a traveler, who is at first indifferent to the old man's melancholy:

> How should I know your true loue,
>   that haue met many a one,
> As I came from the holy Land,
>   that haue come, that haue gone?

But after he is told that "there is none hath her form so diuine on the earth, in the ayr," the traveler reports that he has seen one "with Angell-like face" and wonders why she has gone away. The old man then sadly explains that the desire some call "loue" is not the same as "Love":

> But Loue it is a durable fire,
>   in the mind euer burning:
> Neuer sick, neuer dead, neuer cold,
>   from it selfe neuer turning.

The creation of a dramatic episode in the poem lends an immediacy to the work. Instead of hearing the author tell a moralistic story, the audience hears an indifferent and later sympathetic traveler react to a wise but sad old man. The poem also illustrates through appropriate images an insightful distinction between unselfish love, as understood by the old man, and physical love, as felt by the woman.

In "The Spanish Lady's Love" (GGW, p. 375; sig. H5) Deloney does much the same thing, and the poem is, again, successful. A Spanish lady has fallen in love with her English captor, and when he is ordered home to England, she declares her love:

> Thou has set this present day,
>   my body free:
> But my heart in prison strong,
>   remains with thee.

The noble Englishman tries graciously to persuade her that a soldier's life would not suit her, that he could not afford to maintain her, and that she should marry a Spaniard. But to all his objections, the Spanish lady remains constant in her love for him. When finally the Englishman admits that he has a wife in England, the Spanish lady immediately ceases her suit even though she cannot cease her love:

> Commend me to thy louing Lady,
>   beare to her this chaine of gold,
> And these bracelets for a token,
>   grieuing that I was so bold.
> All my Iewels in like sort
>   beare thou with thee:
> For these are fitting for thy wife,
>   and not for me.

Another poem that is successful primarily because of its use of dialogue is "A pleasant Dialogue Between plaine Truth and Blind Ignorance" (GGW, p. 351; sig. F2v). Blind Ignorance is Catholic, Plaine Truth Protestant; and as we might expect Truth has the better of the debate. But although Truth uses the clear, idiomatic English of Deloney's heroes and Ignorance speaks in the dialect of the rustic, Truth does not easily overwhelm his opponent. Ignorance has remained faithful to Rome because during the days of the "old law" life was better:

> Chill tell thee what, good vellow;
>   beuore the Vriers went hence,
> A bushell of the best wheat
>   was zold for vorteene pence:
> And vorty Eggs a penny,
>   that were both good and new:

> And this che zay my selfe haue zeene
> and yet ich am no Iewe.

When Truth complains that Catholics do not follow the Bible in their doctrines, preferring the foolish mass, Ignorance answers, "Ich care not for this Bible Book,/tis too big to be true." The mass, he continues, cannot be foolish, because it is in Latin, and no one foolish can use Latin.

His ready wit and independent nature allow Ignorance to hold his own in the debate. He admits that the songs of the friars were meaningless to those who did not understand Latin, but, he says, they sounded good and he laments the fact that they are no longer there. He will not follow the new fashion merely because it is the new fashion:

> Ah, ah, che smell thee now, man,
>   che know well what thou art:
> A vellow of new learning,
>   che wis not worth a vart:
> Vor when we had the old Law
>   a mery world was then:
> And euery thing was plenty,
>   among all zorts of men.

Calm and kind throughout, Plaine Truth repeats his theme that the teachings of Christ in the Scriptures must be followed. Finally, and abruptly, Ignorance relents and promises to believe only in the gospel: "And with these subtill Papists/ich haue for euer done." Deloney's predominantly Protestant audience would, of course, have been delighted at the old man's acceptance of truth, and the modern audience does not too much dislike the expected moral ending. The debate is lively and not too one-sided, and Truth never grows too obnoxious in his religious fervor.

Deloney is most effective as a composer of ballads when he is telling a story of great interest or excitement to him, when he is creating a dramatic episode through dialogue, or when he is reflecting upon or reporting about middle-class people and their problems. But because English history and tales of high romance were very popular topics in Elizabethan England, Deloney wrote many ballads dealing with romantic legends or with episodes drawn from the chronicle histories. As a commercial writer, Deloney must have recognized the need to give the public what it wanted: the results are ballads on topics that range from kings and queens to their paramours, from commoners such as Wat Tyler and Jack Straw to important stories in English history such as that of Lady Godiva's famous ride. Of all his extant ballads, more deal with lords and ladies of past history and romance than with any other topic. Most of these ballads, however, are little more than narrative prose paraphrased in meter—the hack work of a writer turning out a certain number of words per day to meet a publisher's deadline.

Deloney does not use historical characters and events as a vehicle for some psychological, social, or philosophical perception; rather, his purpose appears to be, as Francis O. Mann suggests, "to worry a narrative into the compass of a catch."[27] Often Deloney creates his rhyme merely by adding superfluous words and phrases which, although irrelevant to the narrative, usually are not inconsistent with the rest of the poem. In "Virtuous Queen Judith" (GGW, p. 355; sig. F5v), for example, Deloney wants to explain that when Judith understands that her town leaders intend to surrender the children of Israel to the invading Assyrians, she goes home and has her maid bring in her finest clothes so that she can make war against the enemy in her own way. The narrative is presented in the tetrameter lines of the ballad, while the required rhyme is accomplished in the essentially irrelevant trimeter lines:

> When she from them was gotten home,
>   Within her palace gate:
> She called to her chiefest maid
>   That on her then did waite.

The use of words, phrases, or lines merely to fill out a ballad line or to provide an easy rhyme, rather than to further the narrative, is perfectly within the tradition of the ballad; and Deloney's use of irrelevant elements cannot approach the fantastic nonsense syllables of some folk ballads. "Jack the Jolly Tar," for example, ends a four-line stanza with "A whang dang diddle-de-dang, fol-lo-day," to provide a line ending with a sound to rhyme with "lay."

But sometimes in his haste to rhyme, Deloney drives irrelevancy to inconsistency. In his ballad on "The Imprisonment of King Edward the Second" (SH, p. 402; sig. B5v) Deloney tells of Queen Isabel's military victory over her husband. In the first few lines of the poem Edward is referred to as a handsome king and adored husband. Later we are told that "his Queene did him so much despise" that she not only cast him into prison but also had him tortured. To Queen Isabel, Edward is neither "comely" nor "deere," but Deloney's desire for rhyme is greater than his sense of consistency in the story:

> Our comely King her husband deere,
>   Subdued by strength as did appeare,
> By her was sent to prison strange,
>   for having done his countrie wrong.

When dealing with material from the chronicles, Deloney displays little passion for his subject. The fact that he wrote four ballads on the deposition of King Edward II suggests that he had some interest in the subject, but the ballads themselves are mere rehearsals of the events. In "A Song of Queene Isabel" (GGW, p. 313; sig. B7), for example, the narrator explains that Isabel, separated from her husband by the interference of the powerful Spencers, travels to France and Germany to seek help in taking the throne away from Edward. Aided by a German knight, she returns to England and defeats her husband. The Spencers are hanged, the King imprisoned, and the young prince is put on the throne. The narrative emphasizes, if anyone, Queen Isabel, but there is no explanation of the conflict between Isabel and Edward which drove the Queen to rebellion. Isabel turns for aid to her brother, the King of France, who first agrees to help, but then refuses to allow any Frenchman to support her. Deloney does not explain the sudden reversal or the effect it had upon Isabel, except to note "This alteration did greatly grieue the Queene." Isabel seems to be the heroine of one ballad, although it is not clear why Edward is a villain. In the other ballads on the subject—"The Imprisonment of Edward the Second" (SH, p. 402; sig. B5v), "Of King Edward the Second, Being Poysoned" (SH, p. 405; sig. B7v), and "The Lamentation of Matreuers and Gurney" (SH, p. 408; sig. C1v)—Isabel is shown to be a dissembling, cruel woman, for she has her imprisoned husband tortured and killed and then compounds her villainy by banishing the men who, at her direction, murdered the King. What Isabel's motives are for her transition from wronged wife to villain are not clear. She has no Mortimer in the ballads to woo her away from faithful service to Edward as she does in Christopher Marlowe's *Edward II*, nor a Gaveston to envy, and no Mortimer to murder the King.

Others of Deloney's ballads dealing with past history show a similar lack of interest either in the story or in craftsmanship. Whether he is writing of King Edward, King John, Henry I, or Henry II, or of some famous event in English history, Deloney appears content to hammer the prose narrative into some sort of verse as rapidly as possible. Even when he chooses the popular tale of Lady Godiva's famous ride, a story which offers many opportunities for praise of English female resoluteness, description of feminine beauty, analysis of male-female sexual behavior, or lewd jest, Deloney merely takes the story he found in the chronicles and sings it "To the Tune of Prince Arthur died at Ludlow" (GGW, p. 309; sig. B4).

In short, like most poets, Deloney is more effective when he is writing about people and events closest to him. He can do little more with kings and queens than copy their exploits from the chronicles. The one time he tried to portray an historical character in a familiar manner in a ballad—when he tried to describe Queen Elizabeth talking to common people in "On the Want of Corn"—the Lord Mayor of London sought to arrest him for demeaning the Queen. But when he writes about the people he lives with—the common people—and about topics that excite him, he creates ballads that are sometimes specific, well developed, and insightful.

In the novels some of Deloney's songs come naturally from the lips of his characters. These lyrical expressions are usually neither narrative nor philosophical except insofar as they advance the plot or help to explain the personalities of the characters. In *The Gentle Craft, Part II*, for example, Robin illustrates his attitude toward women generally and Long Meg specifically when he says,

> *For this to sweare I dare be bold:*
> *You were a maid at three years old.*
> *From three to foure, fiue, sixe, and seauen,*
> *But when you grew to be eleuen,*
> *Then you began to breed desire;*
> *By twelue your fancy was on fire:*
> *At thirteene yeares desire grew quicke,*
> *And then your maiden-head fell sicke:*
> *But when you came vnto fourteene,*
> *All secret kisses was not seene:*
> *By that time fifteen yeares was past,*
> *I guesse your maiden-head was lost.*
> *And I pray God forgiue me this,*
> *If thinking so I thinke amisse.*
>
> (pp. 147-48; sig. B3)

Meg takes the accusation in good humor because it was offered without malice. Most of the songs sung by the workers in the novels stress the good-natured relationships between the workers in the shops, as in part of the song sung by the weavers in *Jack of Newbury:*

> The Cedar tree indures more stormes,
> > than little shrubs that sprout not hie:
> The Weauer liues more void of harmes,
> > than Princes of great dignitie.
> > > While loue and friendship doth agree,
> > > To hold the bands of amitie.
>
> The Shepheard sitting in the field,
> > doth tune his pipe with hearts delight:
> When Princes march with speare and shield,
> > the poore man soundly sleepes all night.
> > > While loue and friendship doth agree,
> > > To hold the bands of amitie.
> > > > > > (p. 32; sig. F2v)

One of the most delightful of the ballad-singing characters in the novels is the fiddler Anthony Now-now in *The Gentle Craft, Part II.* When the Green King, a shoemaker, becomes bankrupt and is deserted by all his supposed friends because he can no longer do anything for them, Anthony buys him wine and sings him a song of brotherhood:

> When should a man shew himselfe gentle and kinde,
> When should a man comfort the sorrowfull minde?
> > O Anthony now, now, now.
> > O Anthony now, now, now.
> When is the best time to drinke with a friend?
> When is it meetest my money to spend?
> > O Anthony now, now, now.
> > O Anthony now, now, now.
> When goes the King of good fellows away?
> That so much delighted in dancing and play?
> > O Anthony now, now, now.
> > O Anthony now, now, now.
> And when should I bid my Master farewell?
> Whose bountie and curtesie so did excell?
> > O Anthony now, now, now.
> > O Anthony now, now, now.
> > > > > > (p. 205; sig. L1v)

These poems from the novels, and many more like them, reflect Deloney's personal acquaintance with the life of the common man of England, and they are therefore not the bleak and sentimental doggerel he sometimes turned out when writing about kings and queens of past history. If he knew little about how members of the nobility should act, he did have a good idea of the qualities middle-class men and women should have. He writes so often in his novels of successful housewives—Mistress Farmer, the two wives of Jack of Newbury, and the Green King's wife are examples— that one would be surprised not to find among his ballads songs concerning the roles of wives. Of several that he wrote, "Salomon's good houswife" and "Mr. Page's Wife" are the most interesting.

"Salomon's good houswife" (MB, p. 490) is a series of proverbs concerning the good housewife as described in chapter 31 of the *Book of Proverbs*. But the poem is more than merely "a very close paraphrase" of the Bible, as F. O. Mann states.[28] Deloney's sincere admiration of a good wife, so often reflected in his novels, is evident in his description of "a gracious wife." One who finds such a wife, he says, may boast that he has found "The richest treasure on the ground." He characterizes the good housewife as one with diligence, industry, wit, generosity, wisdom, fear of God, and concern for her own and her husband's reputations. Like the Green King's wife, the good housewife aids her husband in his business:

> And while she liues will still procure,
> By true and faithfull industrie,
> T'increase his wealth, and to insure
> His state in all securitie:
>   To seeke his quiet, worke his ease,
>   And for a world no way displease.

Perhaps some autobiography may be found in "Salomon's good houswife." Using the third person throughout most of the poem, in stanza 13 and in only that one stanza Deloney abruptly changes to first person to have himself (rather than husbands generally) praise one particular woman (rather than good housewives generally):

> I know t'is true that more then one
> Good houswife there is to be found:
> But I may say, that thou alone

> Aboue all women dost abound,
>   Yea I protest in all my daies,
>   Thou art the first, and thee ile praise.

Another suggestion that Deloney may have been writing about his own wife is that in his catalogue of qualities of the good housewife, he devotes two stanzas to describing her clothmaking skill and industry. Deloney was, of course, a clothmaker, and the language he uses to describe the craft ("faire," "honor," "worth") accentuates the value of this quality in a wife:

> Her skill doth worke faire Tapistrie,
> With linnen furnish'd of the best:
> Her needle workes do beautifie,
> And she in Scarlet costly drest,
>   When Senators assembled be,
>   Her husbands honor there shall see.
> Her spinning shall her store increase,
> The finest cloth shall yeeld her gaine,
> And dayly profit shall not cease,
> Which her vnidle hands maintaine:
>   Her clothing shall her worth expresse,
>   And Honors years her end possesse.

A very different kind of woman from "Salomon's good houswife" is the subject of "The Lamentation of Mr. Page's Wife" (MB, p. 482). This is probably the best of the journalistic poems, but it is also the one with the most troublesome subject. The ballad, about a woman sentenced to die for the murder of her husband, could have descended into sentimentality of the worst kind, but it does not. Apparently based upon an actual incident in 1590,[29] the ballad presents a moving analysis of the motives and regrets of the young Mrs. Ulalia Page of Plymouth, who, along with her lover, George Strangwidge, murdered Mr. Page.

Ulalia Page's lament is not merely that she must die though still young. While she admits her guilt and the wrongness of her act, she nevertheless argues that parents who force a daughter to marry against her will are also guilty. Ulalia had fallen in love with George Strangwidge, but her father matches her with the old but wealthy Mr. Page. Ulalia therefore faces a life with a man she detests. Ulalia pleads not to be sold to old Page:

> On knees I prayde they would not me constraine;
> With teares I cryde their purpose to refraine;
> With sighes and sobbes I did them often moue,
> I might not wed whereas I could not loue.

But her prayers are in vain. Old Page was a decent enough man ("Cause knew I none I should despise him so"); yet, because he was not young Strangwidge, to Ulalia he appeared as a monster. Deloney is able to evoke sympathy for the desperate young woman by having her reveal a state of near panic. She explains her revulsion for Page in four end-stopped lines which suggest the halting speech and excited breathing of the doomed woman. The stanza ends with an effective metonymy:

> My closen eies could not his sight abide:
> My tender youth did lothe his aged side:
> Scant could I taste the meate whereon he fed:
> My legges did loathe to lodge within his bed.

"The Lamentation of Mr. Page's Wife" is successful primarily because it possesses a degree of unity not often seen in street ballads, because it does not exploit the more sensational aspects of adultery and murder, and because Ulalia's emotions and motives are carefully analyzed. It is true that Deloney adds the usual moral ("Lord! bless our Queene with long and happy life"). These are standard elements in all of Deloney's journalistic ballads, whether the primary subject is the burning of a town or the report that "cruell whippes" to be used by the Spaniards against English men and women had been found on captured Spanish ships. But the emphasis in "The Lamentation of Mr. Page's Wife" is upon the heartsick young woman whose life was made miserable by greedy parents and by an unnatural social custom which allowed women to be treated as chattels.

The subjects of Deloney's ballads are usually dignified enough to attract the attention of judicious readers. Poets like Philip Sidney and George Gascoigne wrote romantic poems, and Samuel Daniel and Michael Drayton borrowed topics from the *Mirror for Magistrates*[30] for their historical poems on subjects similar to Deloney's. But these poets, writing for a more select audience, were able to use metrical and stanzaic patterns inappropriate for the balladeer. Deloney, clearly writing for a bourgeois audience, fitted his words and music to that audience. The public expected the ballads to be sung to familiar tunes, and as a result Deloney delivered his stories to the tune of "the hunt is vp" or "Flying Fame" or "Prince Arthur died at Ludlow" or even "My Valentine." While such restrictions might have reined the wit of a better poet, Deloney nevertheless was successful enough to inherit from Elderton his title, "King" of the ballad writers.

Whether or not Deloney ever had ambitions to achieve a poetic reputation as something other than a balladmaker satisfying the tastes of street crowds is ultimately unanswerable. But his refusal to use merely sensational events for his ballads seems to elevate him at least above the Autolycuses of his day. And on one occasion Deloney left ballads entirely to try his hand at a longer poem of dignified style and matter.

III   Canaans Calamitie, or the Doleful Destruction of Faire Ierusalem

In *Canaans Calamitie* (p. 417) Deloney tells the story of the destruction of Jerusalem by the Roman Titus in A.D. 74, using as sources *de Bello Iudaico* (c. A.D. 75) by Flavius Josephus[31] and *Christs Teares ouer Ierusalem* (1593) by Thomas Nashe. Deloney's most ambitious poem attempts to tell a significant story in a form befitting its moral importance. And in some respects the poem is successful. There is a clear narrative, which includes an understandable conflict, a crisis, and a denouement. The action in the narrative is detailed and generally relevant, and descriptions of characters, setting, and motives are usually, although not always, detailed. His purpose in *Canaans Calamitie* is clearly stated in the note "To the Gentlemen Readers health":

> . . . in reading this Historie, you shall see how soone their state was changed, and the great plagues that followed their peuish and hatefull pride: by whose wofull fall, God graunt vs and all Christians to take example, lest following them in the like sinne, we feele the like smart.
>
> (P.419; sig. A2v)

The moral lesson Deloney finds in the destruction of Jerusalem does not come from Josephus, whose purpose in writing *de Bello Iudaico* was partly political and partly an apology for the Jews and for himself. Josephus, having been captured by the Roman general Vespasian prior to the attack upon Jerusalem, was present at the famous battle as an intermediary for the Romans. Josephus tried to persuade the Jews to surrender, partly because he was aware of the Romans' strength and partly because he detested the zealots, especially John, son of Levi, who through deception gained control over the citizens of Jerusalem. His account of the war assigns the blame for the destruction of Jerusalem to his political enemies, not to either the Jewish people or the official leadership.

Deloney's use of the story as a moral allegory, in which the sins of the people of Jerusalem (or of London in the allegory) are compared to those of the Elizabethans, comes more from Nashe than from Josephus. Referring to the last decade of the sixteenth century as "the dayes of dolor and heauiness," Nashe explains his reason for writing *Christs Teares:* "I suppose it shal not be amisse to write something of mourning, for *London* to harken counsaile of her great Grand-mother, *Ierusalem.*"[32]

Christs Teares is unlike most of Nashe's other works. "The perfect literary showman," as C. S. Lewis calls him, "the juggler with words who can keep a crowd spell-bound by sheer virtuosity,"[33] is in this work apparently attempting a serious subject instead of pamphleteering. The results are, however, not pleasing. The work begins with a long speech by Christ, which is repetitious, vague, and boring. There follows a description of the siege and defeat of Jerusalem in which Nashe is able to resort to shocking subjects and sensational descriptions. Josephus does discuss the famine in the city and reports that those in power among the inhabitants of Jerusalem stole food from the weak. He further reports that "terrible methods of torture" were used to discover where food was hidden, but he does not illustrate the methods. And while Josephus says that the hunger was so great that mothers would pull food from the mouths of infants, nowhere does he describe the ordeal of a Miriam, whose hunger was so great that she killed, roasted, and ate her own son. Miriam appears to be Nashe's invention.

After explaining that the hunger of the Jews was so great that they ate rats, mice, weasels, and even worms and grasshoppers, and that Miriam had "sustained her lyfe a large space by scraping in chaffe and muck-hils for beastes dung,"[34] Nashe gives over the rest of his description of the famine to Miriam's rationalization of why she should eat her son. He follows an admonition to the "mothers of LONDON" to put themselves in Miriam's place with a 148-line soliloquy by Miriam in which she explains in general terms her great need, her son's sure demise, and her desire to protect him and herself from the seditious

Jews. The emotional high point of Nashe's description is handled succinctly and effectively in one short paragraph:

> At one stroke . . . she beheaded him, and when she had done, turning the
> Apron from her own face on his, that the sight might not afreshly distemper
> her, without seeing, speaking, deliberating, or almost thinking any more of
> him, she sod, rost, and powered him; and hauing eaten as much as suffised,
> sette vp the rest.[35]

Nashe ends his book by calling upon London to learn from the errors
of Jerusalem by turning away from pride. For nearly one hundred
pages he moralizes epigrammatically about the vices of London, the
five sons and three daughters of Pride. So generally are the vices portrayed that they are neither frightening nor attractive. Ambition builds
on sand, Avarice is the spur to Ambition, Atheism is drunk on too much
love of the world, and so on. *Christs Teares*, although it occasionally
indicates remote kinship with Nashe's *The Unfortunate Traveller*
(1594), is usually merely unfortunate.[36]

Deloney is surely indebted to Nashe, for he borrows not only the
story generally and the allegorical trappings, but also the story of Miriam in particular. While there are understandable similarities between
Deloney's story and its most immediate source, there are also clear differences. Deloney did not, as he did in drafting many of his ballads on
past history, merely force his source material into meter. He used the
story of the destruction of Jerusalem he got from Josephus and Nashe,
but he altered it to suit his own purposes. And by concentrating upon
the specific elements in the story—a description of the city, the sins of
the people, details of preparation for war, the horrors of famine—
instead of upon Christ's and Nashe's tedious moralizing, Deloney is
more successful than Nashe in calling attention to an historical allegory
warning of the wages of sin.

In preparation for this grand plan, Deloney sets an epic tone by
showing the vastness of his theme and his serious treatment of it:

> Like to a Mourner clad in dolefull black,
> That sadly sits to heare a heauie tale:
> So must my pen proceed to shew the wrack,
> That did with terror *Syon* hill assaile.
> What time *Ierusalem* that Cittie faire,
> Was sieg'd and sackt by great *Vespatians* heire.
>   (lines 1–6)

The city is described as rich, elegant, and beautiful: "In all the world the like might not be seene" (1. 13). The people of Jerusalem, however, are proud and unrepentant, and as a result of their mocking the words of Christ and finally crucifying Him, they are doomed to destruction unless they repent. Forewarnings of the impending punishment are ignored or misunderstood by the Jews; and the prophet Ananias, who warns that unnatural behavior will result in "Woe and destruction," is thrown into a dungeon and whipped. God's retribution comes in the form of the Roman army, led by Titus, son of the Roman emperor Vespasian. He isolates the city, cutting off water and food supplies. When "one seditious Squire" burns the town's stored food supply, the people of Jerusalem are in immediate danger of starvation. Instead of lamenting the sorrows of neighbors and thus repenting, the Jews grow more cruel, stealing from the weak so as to prolong life selfishly. Hearing tales of cannibalism, Titus storms the city, occupies it, and frees the people from the cruel Jewish leaders, who escape. Titus tries to protect the holy temple in the city, but a Jewish attack upon the Romans guarding the temple causes the Romans to retaliate by burning it. Although Titus attempts to extinguish the fire, the temple is destroyed. When the Jewish leaders who had escaped Roman capture grow hungry and surrender, the story is over. Then "to *Rome* the Conqueror went his way" (line 1261), and Deloney is ready to repeat his moral:

> God grant we may our hateful sins forsake,
> And by the Iewes a Christian warning take.
> (lines 1277–78)

The moral does not, however, dominate the poem to such an extent that the story remains abstract. Sin and goodness have here a local habitation and a name. We are told that the timber construction of Jerusalem "was all of precious wood," that there were "pleasant walkes," "pleasant bowers," and "sweet daintie gardens" with "sweetest smelling flowers" (*passim*, lines 21 –36). There is even a bird's-eye view of the city:

> Three stately walles begirt this Citty round,
> Strongly raild vp of gallant squared stone,
> Vnpossible in fight foes should them confound,
> By warlike Engines seized therevpon.

> The spacious gates most glorious to behold,
> Were all gilt ouer, with rich burnisht gould.
>
> (lines 25–30)

Unlike Josephus, Deloney does not comment on the military ability
of the Jews or on the strategy employed by the Romans. Deloney's
emphasis throughout is on the sinfulness of the Jews. Josephus wanted
the Jews to surrender partly because he knew that the Romans were
militarily superior; he describes specific battles, Roman tactics, and
Jewish military blunders. Deloney, on the other hand, treats the
Romans as the avenging hand of God rather than a tactical unit. He
does use specific detail, however, to further his narrative. As the city
prepares for attack, for example, Deloney describes how the pleasures
of peace must give way to the duties of war:

> Instead of Lutes and sweete resounding Vials.
> They sound the Trumpets and the ratling drum,
> Their barbed Steeds they put to diuers tryals,
> How they can manage, stop, carrie, and run:
>   Their cunning harpers now must harnesse beare,
>   Their nimble dauncers war-like weapons weare.
>
> (lines 253–58)

The central part of the poem deals with the effect of the famine
upon the citizens of Jerusalem; here Deloney's reputation for realism
is most warranted. He begins with a description of the general effect
of the famine upon the people:

> When bread was gone, then was he counted blest,
> That in his hand had either cat or dogge,
> To fill his emptie maw: and thus distrest,
> A dozen men would fight for one poore frogge,
>   The fairest Lady lighting one a mouce,
>   Would keepe it from her best friend in the house.
>
> A weazell was accounted a daynty meate,
> A hissing snake esteem'd a Princes dish,
> A Queene vpon a moule might seeme to eate,
> A veanom neawt was thought a wholesome fish:
>   Wormes from the earth were dig'd vp great & small,
>   And poysoned spiders eaten from the wall.
>
> (lines 331–42)

It is true that the superfluous words used to fill out the line are some-what disturbing to the modern reader inescapably influenced by the "new critics." A "hissing snake" is probably no better or worse than a dish than a non-hissing snake, but Deloney needed another iambic foot for his line. At the same time, phrases added to achieve rhyme lead to basically unnecessary verbiage and, sometimes, forced rhyme. "In the house," "great & small," and "from the wall" are used primarily for rhyming, not to add necessary detail. They are, however, a part of the essential realism of Deloney's description of the famine and they add, in varying degrees, color, point, and tone. The use of specific detail in the panoramic view of hunger in the city is impressive.

Had Deloney ceased at this point, his specific description of the elements of life in famine-plagued Jerusalem and his dramatization of the emotions of the mother and child would have effectively created pity for the unlucky Jews. Deloney follows Josephus in blaming Jerusalem's leaders for the suffering of the people. Even the unnatural acts of the starving populace, especially of Miriam, are brought about by the seditious leaders of Jerusalem. But Deloney's purpose is perhaps not merely to move his audience to pity or to allow the general populace to escape blame. For Josephus it is enough, for example, to describe a hunger so intense that it is destructive to decency. If the famine itself is the important element, it is enough to describe a hunger so great that men would eat cats, dogs, or rats. Anyone aware of world hunger problems recognizes that such horrible things have occurred and still do, and one is properly moved to pity. Even to describe a hunger so great that

> Some men with hunger falleth raging mad,
> Gnawing the stones and timber where they walke
> (lines 373–74)

does not so overpower the senses as to create horror in the imagination. But Deloney, like Nashe, does not depict the Jews as merely driven mad by starvation. Driven to hunger by their greedy leaders, the Jews display their sinful nature by their own unnatural acts. Following Nashe, Deloney describes the crudest kind of behavior:

> And other some licks vp the vomit fast,
> Which their sick neighbours in their houses cast.
> (lines 377–78)

This kind of sensationalism is typical of Nashe, but rare in Deloney. When Nashe describes the torture of Zadoch in *The Unfortunate Traveler*, he is trying to shock his audience, not move them to pity. Nashe deals with the story of Miriam's extreme hunger in *Christs Teares ouer Ierusalem*, again for shock purposes. Deloney is usually more subdued. When he describes the murder of Thomas Cole in *Thomas of Reading*, for example, the emphasis is upon the character of Cole rather than upon the details of the murder itself. Occasionally he includes some of the details of historical cruelty in his ballads, as when he describes both the torture and death of Edward II. But nowhere does he approach the grotesque as in *Canaans Calamitie*. Here he out-Nashes Nashe, at least insofar as *Christs Teares* is concerned. Deloney himself seems to fear that he is possibly becoming too sensational when he says "this be all too much" (line 379). But he does not stop. "Nay more than this," he says,

> Iosephus writes, that men and maidens young
> To which of late did scorn brown-bread to touch,
> Sustain'd themselues with one anothers doong.
> (lines 380–82)

Nor does Deloney stop with having Miriam and her son starve to death because they cannot find even a piece of discarded leather to eat. To have done so would have been to cast Miriam and her son as merely pitiful characters caught in circumstances beyond their control. They are pitiful, but they are also culpable. Miriam refuses to let her son gnaw off his fingers or toes because it is "gainst nature." Then calling him "deere child," "ioyfull child," "louing sonne," and "bonny boy," Miriam plunges a sword into her son, cuts him into pieces, roasts part of him, and eats. Her calling him "sweete boy" now takes on meanings that were not heretofore possible. She even admits that while her son was sweet while alive, "Yet sweeter farre, a thousand times thou art" (line 721) now dead and roasted. Deloney thus achieves pity for his characters by having them suffer from the sins of others; and, at the same time, he draws Miriam into the same kind of sin that caused the destruction of Jerusalem by having her commit the most horrible act imaginable.

The story of Canaan's calamity suited Deloney well, as it did Nashe and several ministers of their time, as an allegory of Elizabethan England. The vices of the inhabitants of Jerusalem, vices which brought down God's wrath upon their heads, were alien to the social tradition of England up to the time of Deloney. The Jews' placing of individual desires above the brotherhood of man was, to the medieval and early Renaissance Englishman, a characteristic of beasts, not men. Traditionally, communities and, later, trade guilds fostered the concept of "the public good." W. J. Ashley notes that medieval society "was unlike a modern society aiming at some particular material advantage, in that it entered into a great part of everyday life. Sick guildsmen were visited, and wine and food sent to them from the feasts; brethren who had fallen into poverty were relieved; their daughters were dowered for marriage or the convent; and when a member died his funeral was attended by the brethren and the due rites provided for."[37] This social theory was, however, beginning to be displaced during the last few decades of the sixteenth century because of a changing economic scene.[38] The advancement of the private person marked a new and, to many Englishmen, frightening departure from the codes of social behavior of the past. Robert Greene condemns the new acquisitiveness in English society in his "Quippe for an Upstart Courtier"

> Since men placed their delights in proud looks and brave attire, hospitality was left off, neighbourhood was exiled, conscience was scoffed at, and charity lay frozen in the streets; now upstart gentlemen for the maintenance of that their fathers never looked after, raised rents, racked their tenants, and imposed great fines.[39]

Other writers, including Thomas Nashe, and the dramatists Thomas Dekker, Thomas Middleton, Philip Massinger, Thomas Heywood, and (especially) Ben Jonson satirized and condemned selfishness and greed which were destroying the traditional social morality of England.

Deloney, writing during a period of great economic upheaval and change, doubtless saw in the story of the fall of Jerusalem an allegory for his time. Perhaps the most obvious parallel was found in the story of the famine. Overpopulation, migration to the cities, and the enclosing of agricultural fields for sheep pasturage put a serious strain on the ability of English farmers to raise enough grain to feed the population. Substandard harvests, which occurred from time to time throughout the sixteenth century, caused serious food shortages in London and the larger cities.[40] Harvests were especially bad in the 1590's when Deloney was writing *Canaans Calamitie*. He exhorts his readers to "take example" from the story of the Jews, "lest following them in the like sinne,

we feele the like smart" (p. 419; sig. A2v). Focusing upon the injustices
visited upon Miriam and her son, Deloney alludes to the sins of his own
time, hoping through pity and fear to instruct his audience in the dangers of violating the traditional social morals which he believes had
made England great. He turns to a theme he had used in "The Lamentation of Beccles" (MB, p. 457) and several other ballads to show
how sin against God's law will bring disorder and, therefore, suffering.
In the longer poem, with its freer form, Deloney is able to draw a more
detailed, more thorough, picture of his view of Elizabethan life and
the sins that he believed would bring the downfall of man. Occasionally, in trying to present the real destruction of Jerusalem which was
brought about by the Jews themselves, Deloney follows Nashe's lead
and his own journalistic bent, thus becoming more sensational than his
purposes required. But although Thomas Deloney is still in some
respects "the great ballad maker, T. D.," parts of *Canaans Calamitie*
show unmistakable signs that he is maturing as a writer.

CHAPTER 3

The Prose Works

I Introduction

DELONEY was almost certainly a silk weaver for a large portion of his life. Not only is there external evidence in the contemporary references to Deloney, but there is also the evidence, in his prose works, that he was intimately familiar with the elements of the trade. Nashe's epithet for Deloney, "The Balletting silke-weauer," suggests that he might have worked at both tasks simultaneously, while his works show familiarity with the routine of weavers as well as those of other craftsmen, and with the area of Berkshire, the center of the Elizabethan textile industry.[1] Why Deloney began to write ballads is not certain.

The economic situation in the late sixteenth and early seventeenth centuries was, at best, unsettled. During the Middle Ages the community had been the center of economic life; and as long as the community held together, it was almost completely self-sufficient economically. The medieval trade guilds did not function as trade unions organized to protect the interests of the members; the community itself and the strong traditions that guided it protected the interests of all members of the community. The guilds organized and directed the trades, limiting the number of apprentices, training competent craftsmen, and controlling the quality of the product. If the apprentice or journeyman did his work well, the master profited; and a successful master provided for his workers. Successful guilds insured a comfortable community, which could then provide social and religious services to the people. W. J. Ashley remarks that the guild system "did, and in large measure, succeed in reconciling the interests of consumers and producers."[2] Self-interest and community interest were, therefore, the same in most cases. Since the workers depended upon the community for their economic well-being, they were anxious to keep the community strong. The sick were nursed, the poor relieved, and the downfallen were lifted up.

Social mobility was rare in medieval society. William Cunningham

51

explains that "The ordinary object of ambition was not so much that of rising out of one's grade, but of standing well in that grade; the citizen did not aim at being a knight, but at being warden and master of his gild, or alderman and mayor of his town."[3] There was, in fact, little profit but the name in becoming a knight. Indeed, unless one chose to be a thief, opportunities for rapid individual economic gain were almost nonexistent in the medieval community. A worker might move from one community to another to find more excitement or a somewhat better standard of living, but in smaller market towns one community was economically pretty much like the next.[4] As long as foreign trade or exploitation was not well developed, no source of ready wealth existed to tempt individuals to gamble the security of one community for the chance to acquire quick personal riches elsewhere.

The late sixteenth and early seventeenth centuries saw a rapid change from the traditional economic system to capitalism. L. C. Knights points out that a capitalistic economy depends upon two basic elements: "the existence of a wider market than the medieval local community" and "an adequate supply of money."[5] These two elements began to emerge early in the sixteenth century insofar as the clothing trade was concerned because foreign markets and foreign money were available for English cloth. Cloth accounted for seventy per cent of the total English exports around the year 1500,[6] and the cloth industry continued to be of major importance into the seventeenth century, when the Privy Council recognized it as "the noblest and richest manufacture of this kingdom."[7] Friis reports that "At the beginning of the seventeenth century the cloth exports of London alone, which were about 130,000 cloths annually, exceeded the average exported from the whole of England during the last years of the reign of Henry VIII."[8]

A seemingly inexhaustible supply of money coming into England, however, changed the economic structure to one in which, according to Knights, "Money and competition," not consideration for the welfare of the community or the quality of goods, "were becoming the prime movers of economic life."[9] The introduction of American gold and silver into the European economy provided riches which attracted so many entrepreneurs that the English economy was in time seriously affected.[10]

This economic boom period brought about a great many exciting artistic, educational, cultural, and social opportunities in England. But it was not without its costs. The medieval economic system, with its stable local markets, had given way to a national capitalistic economy which fluctuated more severely and more often. The new money and a great many other considerations had caused severe inflation, while the market fluctuations had caused massive unemployment. J. M. Keynes reports that prices around the year 1650 were approximately three times what they were in 1500,[11] and the greatest decade of inflation was the 1590s. Although England under Elizabeth was "economically prosperous," according to Knights, "that prosperity was far from being universally shared."[12] The long war with Spain closed traditional markets on the Continent for English cloth, causing "much unemployment in the clothing trade."[13] A dearth of corn and outbreaks of the plague in London during the 1590s caused "the whole trade of the city," according to W. R. Scott, to be "much impaired and its traffic greatly diminished."[14] The plague was especially bad in the major clothing center of Norwich during the 1580s and 1590s.

The economic problems of the 1590s were caused by a complex series of circumstances. The enclosure movement, for example, fenced off large areas of English land which had been used by tenant farmers to produce grain and vegetables. Land owners enclosed the land because wool production was more profitable to them than rents paid by tenant farmers, but the enclosures clearly displaced many hundreds of tenants, causing overpopulation in the cities, and reduced significantly the production of food.[15] Enclosures therefore contributed to the unemployment, famine, and inflation already present in England. These conditions helped to spawn even more social problems, such as an increase in the number of rogues and vagabonds.[16] There were, in addition, sharp reductions in the number of cloth exports during the last two decades of the sixteenth century, exports which were of major economic importance to England during the sixteenth and seventeenth centuries.[17] This decline in trade, caused by many factors—including economic problems, government regulations, and the war with Spain—contributed to unemployment, which coincided with a scarcity of food exacerbated by enclosures and poor harvests. The result was that prices rose to their highest levels so that even people who had jobs could not afford to buy food.[18]

The complex economic situation existing during the sixteenth and seventeenth centuries, of which I have sketched merely the barest essentials, almost certainly helped to inspire Deloney's literary activities. The inspiration probably had two sources. First, the problem of unemployment in the clothing industry perhaps affected Deloney directly: he may have had no other job. Second, as a businessman

Deloney clearly was aware of economic problems affecting trade, as his ballads and prose works show. In 1595 he had been arrested for complaining about unfair trade practices on the part of foreign weavers. In 1596 he was in legal trouble for writing a ballad dealing with one of the issues involved in the economic instability, his "Ballad on the Want of Corn."

Many of Deloney's ballads and all of his prose works deal with social problems. In his prose works especially, he draws a world much like his own: full of problems and opportunities. He peoples this world with characters who can solve the problems (unemployment, avarice, thievery, various economic ills, jealousy, class snobbery, and the like) and take advantage of the opportunities (business profits, ample good food, attractive clothing, economic security). Deloney's model for a successful life is the ordered universe as reflected in the great chain of being. This chain begins at the foot of God and descends to include all things. The universe is, according to Ulysses in Shakespeare's *Troilus and Cressida*, a tuned instrument which operates in harmony:

> The heavens themselves, the planets, and this centre
> Observe degree, priority, and place,
> Insisture, course, proportion, season, form,
> Office, and custom, in all line of order.
> (I.iii.85–88)

Peaceful, productive society reflects this cosmic order:

> How could communities,
> Degrees in schools, and brotherhoods in cities,
> Peaceful commerce from dividable shores,
> The primogenity and due of birth,
> Prerogative of age, crowns, sceptres, laurels,
> But by degree stand in authentic place?
> Take but degree away, untune that string,
> And hark what discord follows.
> (I.iii,103–110)

Sixteenth-century England found herself between two worlds: the ordered world of accepted classes, roles, behavior, and dress and the new commercial world which offered profit as a motive for actions. E. M. W. Tillyard suggests that "The new commercialism was hostile to medieval stability."[19] This new world had been both good and bad to

Deloney. Since he was a silk weaver, the new commercialism offered him the opportunity to direct his own destiny, to profit from his skill and industry. But it lacked the security of the medieval model. Since profit was the motive, irresponsible leaders, thieves, con artists, parasites, and those who engaged in unfair business practices could drain profits from the industrious businessman. Deloney's solution was to merge the two worlds, to show that the profit motive can offer success and security when it operates within the general structure of the moral order of the universe. The commercial world he found himself in certainly was not secure; unemployment, inflation, and hunger were some of the social problems facing the middle-class merchant of the late sixteenth century. In his novels, therefore, Deloney created models for the merging of the two worlds.

It may be that Deloney turned to writing during a period of unemployment as a silk weaver. Thomas Nashe, declaring that Deloney's muse had ever been fed on small beer, claimed that during the dearth of 1596 his looms were stopped altogether. Sounding somewhat like the poet's friend in A. E. Housman's "Terence, This Is Stupid Stuff," Nashe reports that Deloney had stopped writing "merrie" poems and begun producing ballads prophesying doom:

—as Thomas Deloney, the Balletting Silke-Weauer, hath rime inough for all myracles, and wit to make a Garland of Good will, more than the premisses, with an epistle of Momus and Zylus; whereas his Muse, from the first peeping foorth, hath stood at Liuery at an Alehouse whispe neuer exceeding a penny a quart, day or night, and this deare yeare, together with the silencing of his looms, scarce that; he being constrained to betake him to carded Ale; whence it proceedeth that, since Candlemas or his Igge of John for the King, not one merrie Dittie will come from him but the Thunder-bolt against Swearers, Repent, England, repent, and the strange judgments of God.[20]

While it is possible that Deloney could have had trouble earning a living as a weaver during the last decade of the sixteenth century,[21] it is unlikely that his own unemployment alone caused him to turn to a literary career. His first known work, "A Declaration Made by the Archbishop of Collen Upon the Deede of His Mariage" (p. 273), is an anti-Catholic tract spawned more by the righteous indignation of a staunch Protestant than by a desire for a quick profit. On the other hand, his journalistic, historical, and romantic ballads, although they show an occasional flash of personal sympathy on the part of the author

toward his subject, were generally created for a popular market. Deloney's shift from silk weaver to writer was gradual, and the reasons
appear to be complex. A number of elements—social, economic, and
personal—were surely involved.

Deloney never completely deserted the ballads for which he was
famous during his own lifetime, but in 1596 he did turn his energies
to writing prose. It may be that his close brush with imprisonment
caused him to decide upon the less risky genre of historical prose,
where he might carry on his social and economic criticism under the
guise of historical allegory. More likely, however, with the economic
hard times of the last decade of the sixteenth century, Deloney, a practical and inveterate storyteller, saw a chance to earn a living by doing
something he liked to do in a medium of growing popularity. Whatever his reasons for abandoning his loom and turning to prose, the
results are important. Although he may have been known to his contemporaries as a balladmonger, his modern reputation properly rests
upon his four major prose works.

No one can argue that Deloney was a polished novelist by modern
standards. His four works of fiction show little desire for the kind of
unity we expect to find in what most scholars following the modern
critic Ian Watt[22] would call a novel. His *Thomas of Reading* has for
its central dramatic emphasis the murder of Thomas Cole of Reading,
but the story is by no means Thomas Cole's exclusively. The work follows the lives of nine clothiers "famous throughout all England" as
they attend to their domestic, social, and business duties. The major
unifying element in the work is that the nine clothiers know each other
and gather occasionally in London. Otherwise, they lead separate lives.
Similarly, the first part of *The Gentle Craft* consists of three stories
tied together only in the loosest sort of way. The story of St. Hugh and
St. Winifred tells how shoemakers' tools came to be called "St. Hugh's
Bones." The second story tells of two young princes who, in banishment, become shoemakers, but although they use "St. Hugh's bones,"
they have nothing to do with the St. Hugh-St. Winifred episode. The
third story involves the rise of the shoemaker Simon Eyre to fortune
and fame, but this episode is not related to the other two, except that
Eyre is a shoemaker. The second part of *The Gentle Craft* also contains three separate stories related to each other only because shoemakers are the protagonists. Even *Jack of Newbury*, which is the most
unified of Deloney's prose works, contains episodes from history, jest

books, *novelle,* and romances that fit only very roughly into the story of the protagonist.

The prose fiction Deloney writes is probably closer to what Northrop Frye identifies as the romance than to the novel.[23] His characters are less "real" than those of Dostoyevsky, Hemingway, or even Defoe, because Deloney rarely analyzes the personalities of his characters, especially of his heroes, as novelists do. On the other hand, his characters are more "real," have more clearly developed personalities, than do the characters in the prose romances written by Philip Sidney, Robert Greene, or Thomas Lodge. Fitting neatly into neither the category of the novel nor the romance, Deloney's prose works are referred to variously by literary critics as "romances," "novels," or the more general "prose fiction." Since, as Frye points out, "'Pure' examples of either form are never found,"[24] the question of what to call Deloney's prose works seems to be of little importance. The phrase "Elizabethan novel" perhaps best describes what Deloney is writing, and that is the designation I prefer. But if he is to be judged by the same criteria as a modern novelist the judgment will be unfair, for his intention, as far as we can determine from reading his works, was not the same as that of the modern novelist. He created heroes who were like men rather than men who were like heroes, and he tells his stories in episodes with little regard for any except thematic unity. His purpose in writing prose fiction is more akin to that of Thomas More in *Utopia* than that of a modern novelist, for Deloney creates an ideal society by attacking social problems through their economic causes.[25] What he shares with modern novelists, or shows them the way to, is his concern with the importance of the lives and work of middle-class men and women. Deloney's realism is not so much in his plots, which are romantic, or in his characters, many of whom are also romantic, but in the problems he designs for his characters to face.

Deloney's lack of external unity does not indicate that there is no artistry in his works. For Deloney, the scene is the narrative unit,[26] and within his episodes, it is obvious that he molds his scenes with great care. Furthermore, his characterization is clear, consistent, and complete. The problems his characters face are those of people who must daily keep shop, make shoes that fit, lobby for professional interests, and get along with their wives and colleagues. Deloney's imagery is often as homespun as his characters, but it does help him clarify his stories. As for his language, Deloney is no Lyly, and Euphues himself would have been thought a great dunce by Deloney's characters for all his ornamented speech, because he could not weave or make shoes or do anything else of practical value.

The loose form of Renaissance prose fiction is puzzling to those of us accustomed to modern novels. And to be sure, Deloney's prose is primarily about middle-class customs and ideas. But here is the street life of the Renaissance and, to some extent, of today. Deloney's work is often overlooked because it is overshadowed by other Elizabethans: Spenser, Sidney, Shakespeare, Jonson, Marlowe, and Webster. But it is also overlooked by academicians because, like Robert Browning's Prior in "Fra Lippo Lippi," we often think that middle-class life is too mundane for art. As Watt makes clear, however, the English novel originates in and is supported financially by the middle class.[27] To be sure, the University Wit Robert Greene dismissed Deloney's works as "triviall trinkets and threedbare trash,"[28] but then it was Greene who dismissed Shakespeare as "an upstart Crow." Deloney's characters are interesting people who are full of life; his imagery is clear, appropriate, and fresh; and his love of and ability to use language is obvious in his works. Llewelyn Powys said in 1933, "In all English literature no writer has been more neglected than Thomas Deloney."[29]

Although it is certain that Deloney did not turn to prose fiction until 1596, much less certain is the specific order in which his works appeared. Entered in the Stationers' Register are *Jack of Newbury* on March 7, 1597, and "a booke called *the gentel crafte* intreating of Shoomakers" on October 19, 1597. The latter entry almost certainly refers to the first part of *The Gentle Craft*, since no distinction is there made between a first and a second part.

Few scholars doubt that, of Deloney's four prose works, *Jack of Newbury* was published first.[30] Probably appearing in 1596 or early 1597, *Jack* was followed in rapid succession by the other three novels, but which came second continues to puzzle scholars. In the introduction to *Jack of Newbury* Deloney promised that if "worthy Clothiers," to whom he had dedicated the work, found his efforts acceptable, "it shall moue mee shortly to set to your sight the long hidden History of *Thomas of Redding, George of Glocester, Richard of Worcester,* and *William of Salisbury,* with divers other" (p. 2; sig. A2v). If it can be assumed that Deloney made good his promise to publish another book dealing with clothiers before turning his attention to shoemakers, then we must agree that he wrote and published three short novels in the space of one year. Francis O. Mann believes differently, saying that "after writing *Jacke of Newberie* he left the weavers for a while to deal with the shoemakers, and only returned to them again in *Thomas of Reading*, written in 1598 or 1599."[31] Deloney's American editor, Merritt E. Lawlis, accepts Mann's suggestion, listing the order of publication as *Jack of Newbury; The Gentle Craft, Part 1; The Gentle Craft, Part 2;* and *Thomas of Reading.* Lawlis does admit, however, that "in the absence of first editions and contemporary references one cannot be certain."[32]

The major reason *Thomas of Reading* is usually considered Deloney's last novel is that it is the most sophisticated of the four, at least from the modern point of view. In its use of a single character as a unifying principle, however, it is closer to *Jack of Newbury* than either part of *The Gentle Craft.* Since all four of the novels were written in no more than four years, speculations that Deloney may have "matured" into a sophisticated writer on a chronological schedule perhaps should not be taken too seriously. Structurally, *Jack of Newbury* is superior to the two parts of *The Gentle Craft,* and *Jack of Newbury* almost certainly came first. It should not be impossible to believe, I think, that Deloney's most sophisticated work was written second, with *The Gentle Craft,* I and II, coming last.

The speculations of both Mann and Lawlis which place *Thomas of Reading* last in the canon have the advantage of spacing the four novels evenly over the last four years of the author's life. But such speculations deny Deloney's own stated intentions. First, Deloney promised in the dedication of *Jack of Newbury* "shortly" to deliver another story dealing with clothiers, especially mentioning Thomas of Reading. There is no clear evidence that he did not immediately deliver his promise. Second, in the dedication of *The Gentle Craft, Part 2,* Deloney promised a third part in which he would continue his tales of shoemakers. His death in 1600 prevented him from fulfilling that promise, but his intention was clear. According to his own stated plans and other evidence, therefore, it is reasonable to assume that the novels were written and published in the following order: *Jack of Newbury* (1596 or 1597); *Thomas of Reading* (1597); *The Gentle Craft, Part 1* (1597); *The Gentle Craft, Part 2* (1598).[33]

II Jack of Newbury

A *The Sources*

Deloney's sources for *Jack of Newbury* are primarily the history and legends of the famous citizen of Newbury, which was and is a busy, thriving community some forty miles west of London. John Smallwood the elder, alias John Winchcombe, had come to Newbury from Winchcombe, in Gloucestershire, a town also known for its extensive clothing trade. As every modern citizen of Newbury knows, John Winchcombe was apprenticed to a wealthy clothier and so distinguished himself as intelligent, hard-working, and honest that, upon his master's death, he was chosen by the widow first to manage the business and later to be her husband and thus own it.

The success of John Winchcombe caused him to become a popular hero widely known as Jack of Newbury, called by Thomas Fuller "the most considerable clothier without fancy and fiction England ever beheld."[34] So important to the economy of England were the clothing industry in general and John Winchcombe's mills in particular that in 1516 and again in 1518 King Henry VIII visited Newbury, staying overnight in the home of the famous clothier. Part of Winchcombe's house, including the room Henry VIII slept in, still graces the town of Newbury on Northbrook Street. The lower part of the house, now remodeled, today houses, appropriately enough, a clothing shop.

Deloney's detailed knowledge of the streets, buildings, suburbs, and families of Newbury can only mean that he lived in Newbury for a time.[35] For example, in Chapter I, the widow instructs her man John to go with her to "Saint *Bartholmewes* Chappell." The chapel, which housed Saint Bartholomewes Grammar School, is commemorated by a tablet on the south wall of the present-day church, which was built during the first half of the sixteenth century. The church, St. Nicholas of Newbury, dominates the town and would have been well known to any resident of Newbury. Jack of Newbury is commemorated in the building by brass plaques, carved bosses, stained-glass windows, and the tomb of Jack and his first wife, Alice.

Although *Jack of Newbury* is drawn primarily from tradition, Deloney embellishes the story by inserting episodes and anecdotes gathered from various other sources. The story of how Jack's first wife, being locked out of the house for staying out too late, tricks Jack into coming outside where he is then locked out by her, is in most respects the same story told by Boccaccio of Tofano and his wife in the fourth story, seventh day, of *The Decameron*. The episode of Benedick's wooing of Joan is similar to a number of stories in folktales, literature, and jest books. Benedick's attempt to make secret and unlawful love to Joan and his being exposed to public ridicule are very close to "The Miller's Tale" of Chaucer and to Boccaccio's story of Friar Alberto, who disguises himself as the Angel Gabriel and tricks Mistress Lisetta into going to bed with him, in the second story, fourth day, of *The Decameron*. The substitution of the pig for Joan is nothing more than a variation of many such stories available to Deloney, especially the ninth story, third day, of *The Decameron*, in which Gillette of Narbonne marries Bertrand against his will and is forced to substitute herself for a mistress secretly in her husband's bed in order to get pregnant: Shakespeare also uses this popular plot of substitution in both *Much Ado About Nothing* and *All's Well That Ends Well*. Deloney so liked the device that he used another variation of it in the last episode in the novel, concerning Sir George and the maiden Joan, who is disguised as the widow Loveless.

Other elements in the novel indicate that Deloney had read, or was at least aware of, a wide variety of literature from France, Italy, and England.[36] But, as Mann points out, Deloney needed as his sources for *Jack of Newbury* nothing other "than his own acquaintance with the floating mass of popular Elizabethan literature."[37]

B *The Plot*

In the days of King Henry VIII, John Winchcombe, an honest, hardworking, generous, and personable young weaver of Newbury, is respected by rich and poor. At the death of his master, the widowed Dame first makes John manager of the weaving business and later marries him. After a period of adjustment, the two prosper and live happily until the Dame dies, leaving Jack wealthy and the sole master of the business.

Jack chooses as his new wife not a rich or noble woman, but one of his workers who has proved her worth in the business. Soon after the wedding, James IV of Scotland invades England while King Henry VIII is out of the country. The Queen orders Jack to send six men to help make up an army, but he outfits one hundred and fifty in handsome uniforms and leads them against the invaders. Although the enemy is defeated before Jack and his men arrive to do battle, the Queen honors Jack for his loyalty.

When King Henry VIII returns to England and is riding through Berkshire, Jack and his men guard an ant hill beside a road the King will travel. Jack explains to the King that the industry of England, like that of the ants, must be defended from the lazy people who would live off the workers. The King praises Jack's ingenuity and concern and promises to come to the aid of the clothiers. Will Sommers, the King's jester, meanwhile, is dallying with the girls who operate Jack's looms. He tries to outwit them, but he finds himself forced to eat with the pigs because of his boldness.

Later, an economic depression in England has diminished the clothing trade and increased unemployment. Jack and other representatives of the clothing industry travel to London to appeal to the King for relief. The King decrees that the merchants be allowed unrestricted trade and, after a delaying tactic by Cardinal Wolsey, during which time Jack is jailed, the decree is finally published, causing trade to improve. The poor are put back to work, and the clothing industry prospers.

Because Newbury is prosperous, both English and foreign noblemen often come to buy cloth or to visit. One such visitor, an Italian merchant named Benedick, falls in love with one of Jack's servants, Joan. Joan spurns his love, mainly because his use of English is crude, and her kinsman insults him when Benedick forces his suit. To get revenge, Benedick tries to seduce the wife of Joan's kinsman. But the tables are turned on the foreigner when he is tricked into getting into bed with a drugged sow. He leaves Newbury before daybreak.

Mistress Winchcombe's neighbor, Mistress Franke, advises the young housewife not to feed her servants such good food. When Nan takes the older woman's advice, Jack upbraids his wife, telling her not to "meddle with such light braind huswives."

Jack goes to London on business, where he has a chance meeting with Randoll Pert, a former London draper, who had declared bankruptcy and been put in jail by his debtors. Pert, recently released from jail, runs from Jack because he is afraid Jack will demand the £500 he still owes. Jack, however, catches up to Pert, has him sign a note for the money to be paid when Pert becomes Sheriff of London, buys him new clothes, and sets him up in the clothing business. Pert prospers, becomes Sheriff, and pays Jack the £500.

While Jack is absent from Newbury, Mistress Franke is bold enough to visit Nan. The young wife is not at home, and Mistress Franke stays to drink wine and condemn the Winchcombes to the servants. When she passes out from drink, the servants hire a "Clowne from Greeneham" to carry her in a basket around town to see if anyone knows her. The sight of the drunken woman in the basket is amusing to the townsfolk, but not to her husband, who boxes her ear and drags her into the house.

Another guest in the Winchcombe house is Sir George Rigley, who takes notice of Jack's servant, Joan. Promising to marry her, the knight works his will on the young girl, who soon finds herself pregnant; but Sir George denies responsibility. Jack, knowing that the knight wants to make a favorable marriage, tells him of a beautiful, young, wealthy widow and urges him to marry her. Sir George hastens to marry "Mistress Loveless," but when he discovers he has married the pregnant Joan, he is angry. Jack delivers a moral sermon which causes the knight to repent and welcome Joan as his wife.

C Analysis

Deloney's primary purpose in *Jack of Newbury* is to show that the hard-working clothiers are in tune with the moral and ethical order of the universe and are, therefore, happy and valuable members of society. Deloney emphasizes that it is Jack's essential honesty, industry, and devotion to duty that gave him his first social and economic rewards. Deloney creates a picture of a strong England, weakened by the pompous, the lazy, the profligate, but strengthened by its most basic industry and those who toil in it. In the foreword to *Jack of Newbury* Deloney asserts that "Among all manual Arts used in the Land, none is more famous for desert, or more beneficial to the Commonwealth, than is the most necessary Art of Clothing" (p. 2; sig. A2). Throughout the work Deloney illustrates that assertion.

E. D. Mackerness believes that Deloney's intent in *Jack of Newbury* and elsewhere is to support social conformity, to please the aristocracy by picturing the workers as simple, happy children who do not have to worry about serious problems of running the church and state. Deloney, in his view, is a propagandist for the government.[38] The new commercialism put a severe strain upon the social structure in sixteenth-century England. Peter Clark and Paul Slack show that "a growing and open polarization" occurred "between an increasingly pampered, narrow elite and the large army of destitute poor."[39] Riots were often the common man's method of retaliating against a system in which he had no effective voice. Lawrence Stone explains that one method the aristocracy used to calm the masses and maintain the status quo was to argue that God had established the classes and that the poor should accept God's will uncomplainingly.[40]

Despite Mackerness's opinion, Deloney's purpose in both his ballads and his novels is to criticize the social and political ills of his society and to offer remedies for these ills by constructing models for a healthy commonwealth. The middle-class citizen in Deloney's model is as important in society as the monarch and more important than those of the titled aristocracy who contribute nothing to the commonwealth. This commonwealth idea is described by Arthur B. Ferguson:

> On the face of it, the ideal of the commonwealth was little more than a vigorous and impassioned restatement of orthodox medieval theory. At its center is the political body, divinely ordained in a form analogous to the natural body, each part having its appointed function to perform for the good of the whole organism. From it radiate a number of important implications. Private interests must be subordinated to those of the community. Indeed if the moral attitude of the individual man is what it should be, if that is, he is moved by Christian charity and a true sense of duty, his interests will never conflict with those of the community. Only if he is moved by pride, avarice, or any other of the vicious drives inherent in his corrupted nature will he pursue his private interest to the detriment of the common "wealth."[41]

Such is Deloney's model. King Henry VIII and Queen Catherine, the monarchs in *Jack of Newbury,* fit Deloney's commonwealth model. They rule, not autocratically, but with a sincere interest in and love of the English working class. When Cardinal Wolsey imprisons Jack and other of the clothiers, the Duke of Somerset warns Wolsey to release them, "for you may perceiue (quoth the Duke) how highly the King esteemes men of that Faculty" (p. 46; sig. H3v).

The King "esteemes men of that Faculty" because, according to Deloney, he recognizes the importance of clothiers to the commonwealth. Visiting Jack in Newbury, the King perceives "what a great number of people were by this one man set on worke." Speaking of the clothing industry, the King tells Jack, "No trade in all the Land was so much to bee charished and maintained as this" (p. 36; sig. G1v). The autocratic Cardinal Wolsey, himself the son of a butcher, who exercises his powers for personal reasons, dislikes Jack and views with disdain the rising influence the common clothiers have with the King. Wolsey insists that Jack's elaborate praise of the King is for self-serving reasons:

> . . . the fellow of this house, hee hath not stucke this day to vndoe himselfe, onely to become famous by receiuing of your Maiesty: like *Herostratus* the Shoomaker that burned the Temple of *Diana,* onely to get himself a name, more than for any affection he beares to your Grace.
>
> (p. 30; sigs. F1-F1v)

The profit motive, says Wolsey, motivates Jack. If the merchants were to be asked to tax themselves to support any of the "waightie affaires of the Common-wealth and state of the Realme" (p. 30; sig. F1v), they would complain bitterly. The King, Deloney's wise, selfless governor of an orderly state in an orderly universe, knows better. Loving his subjects, concerned with the prosperity of all segments of the commonwealth, and recognizing the benefits of business to the good of all, Henry VIII explains the structure of the commonwealth and the clothiers' place in it:

As the Clergy for the soule, the Souldier for defence of his country, the lawyer to execute iustice, the Husbandman to feede the belly: so is the skilfull Clothier no lesse necessary for the cloathing of the backe, whom we may reckon among the chiefe Yeomen of our Lande: and as the christall sight of the Eye is tenderly to be kept from harmes because it gives the whole body light: so is the Clothiers whose cunning hand provides garments to defend our naked parts from the Winters nipping frost.

(pp. 44–45; sig. H2v)

The government, therefore, will do whatever is necessary to encourage free enterprise. Wolsey, arguing that he must maintain standards, delays implementation of the order as long as he can, but in Deloney's model commonwealth Wolsey is less influential than the productive workers. In this utopia the interests of the King and of the workers are identical: class differences, pride, and business profits are all of less importance than a healthy commonwealth.

John Winchcombe is, to be sure, a businessman interested in profits. He marries a rich widow, and his daily work is to increase his wealth. But Jack's responsibilities to society are as carefully developed by Deloney as the King's are. For example, Jack is attractive to the discerning widow because in his work she found him "carefull and diligent" (p. 3; sig. A2v) and in his general demeanor generous, pleasant, and moderate: "hee would alwaies keepe himselfe in comely and decent apparell: neyther at any time would hee bee ouercome in drinke, but so discreetly behaue himselfe with honest mirth, and plesant conceits, that he was euery Gentlemans companion" (p. 3; sig. A2). Jack is made foreman of the business, and later he becomes master; but he earns his promotions.

As a successful businessman, Jack continues his allegiance to the commonwealth by supporting the monarch when England is threatened. When James of Scotland invades England and Jack equips the one hundred and fifty soldiers and leads them to the Queen, many of the noblemen who had gathered at the order of the Queen were envious because, as Deloney tells us, "the best nobleman in the country would scarce haue done so much" (p. 23; sig. D4v). The Queen also praises Jack for his sense of responsibility:

Welcome to mee Iack of Newberie (said the Queene) though a Clothier by trade, yet a Gentleman by condition, and a faithfull subiect in heart: and if thou chance to haue any sute in Court, make account the Queene will bee thy friend, and would to God the King had many such Clothiers.

(p. 24; sig. E1)

Jack's sense of responsibility to the commonwealth is not limited to supporting a king who protected business interests. What the king is to his subjects, Jack is to his employees and to others of his profession who are dependent on him. Jack rules his empire, not as an autocrat, but as a benevolent monarch interested in the welfare of his fellows. At one point when he becomes too paternalistic, his first wife reminds him of the partnership nature of marriage and, by implication, of the commonwealth and business. Complaining that Jack was acting "like a Iudge on the Bench" (p. 18; sig. D1), she shows him that true power comes from wisdom, not physical force. He learns, therefore, not to attempt to rule his wife or anyone else with an iron hand. When his second wife, on the advice of the old gossip, begins to skimp on the meals she serves the workers, Jack explains that "Empty platters makes greedy stomachs, and where scarcity is kept, hunger is nourished" (p. 56; sig. K2v).[42] In all his actions, Jack is the model for his workers and, presumably, Deloney's readers.[43]

Even when Henry VIII attempts to make Jack a knight, Jack refuses the offer:

O my dread Soueraigne (said Iacke) honour and worship may bee compared to the Lake of *Laethe*, which makes men forget themselues that taste thereof: and to the end I may still keepe in minde from whence I came, and what I am, I beseech your Grace let mee rest in my russet coat, a poore Clothier to my dying day.

(p. 38; sig. G2v)

"Poore Clothier" must be taken as a class, different from "honored knight," because Jack is certainly not financially poor. He is a clothier, an important part of an ordered cosmos, and he does not want to untune his good life by forgetting who he is. When others in his class make mistakes, Jack is therefore able to help them set their lives straight again. He tells the King, "these are the labouring Ants whom I seeke to defend, and these be the Bees which I keepe: who labour in this life, nor for our selues, but for the glory of GOD, and to do service to our dread Souereigne" (p. 38; sig. G2v).

One such "Ant" is Randoll Pert, the bankrupt draper in London. That Pert does succeed in business, become Sheriff of London, and repay his debt to Jack is pure romance, but it is Jack's attitude that is important here. Pert is no good to the commonwealth (and therefore to Jack) if he is in jail. Jack recognizes the pragmatic nature of his actions; he says, "if hee be not able to pay me when he is at liberty, he will neuer be able to pay mee in prison" (p. 58; sig. K3). Jack's motive is self-interest, but it is enlightened self-interest. What he does is right for the commonwealth as well as for himself.

The minor characters in the novel are used to support the commonwealth theme in one way or another. Will Sommers, the King's jester, is the kind of buffoon Shakespeare used to increase the festivities in his comedies, and Deloney uses him for the same purpose. But perhaps more important, Will's conflict with Jack's female weavers allows Deloney to show the wit and resourcefulness of working women. That they gain the upper hand against Will in front of the King's retinue— and gain the approval of the King and Queen—illustrates the importance of these women in the scheme of things. In the episode, while Jack is busy entertaining Henry VIII and instructing the King in the benefits to the country of "the most necessary Art of Clothing," Will is engaged in the less serious business of making fun of the maidens who work in Jack's shop. An element of crude slapstick is added to the narrative when the resourceful maidens bind and gag the jester and flap him in the face with a bag of wet dog droppings. Will gets his final deserts when he is compelled to feed the swine and dine on the same swill himself. The rebuke delights the King and Queen and pleases the audience.

With the characters Master Benedick and Sir George Rigley Deloney introduces personalities to serve as foils for Jack. They are minor villains who try to take advantage of honest people and who pay for their actions. When Benedick, the Italian merchant, attempts to make love to one of Jack's young maids, her kinsman John warns him to stay away from her. Benedick's first thought is of revenge, as one might expect of an Italian in Elizabethan England; and he attempts to seduce John's wife, Gillian. The respectable John has the best of the encounter, however, when he tricks Benedick into going to bed with a sow pig. Much to the amusement of the neighbors, Benedick leaps from the bed thinking that he has embraced the devil. Benedick is thus punished for attempting to bring chaos into ordered family life. Jack, interestingly, is not involved in this episode as the defender of ants, any more than he was in the episode involving Will Sommers and the weavers. John, the head of the family unit, defends the concept of order here as Jack does in the other episodes. Noteworthy, too, are the wisdom and integrity of the two women, who are so much a part of the moral order exemplified by Jack that they cannot be wooed away by mere wealth. The fact that Benedick is a foreigner is important, too. As I have noted, the influx of refugees into sixteenth-century England was one of the causes of the social and economic problems central to Deloney's writings. Deloney, who had been jailed for complaining about unfair business practices, was not kindly disposed toward even those foreigners who could speak English fluently.

In a later episode Sir George Rigley gets one of Jack's maids pregnant and refuses to marry her. Since such a lack of responsibility is alien to Jack's philosophy of right living, Jack himself intervenes to trick the knight into wooing and wedding the girl, whom he believes to be a wealthy widow. Jack chides Sir George for thinking Joan a "lewd paltry thing" (p. 64; sig. L3v) and assures him that the girl is at least his equal, an idea which acquires credibility when Sir George believes Joan to be a lady when he sees her wearing a lady's clothing. Sir George is made to see the rightness of Jack's actions, and even the King agrees that justice has been done. Neither Sir George nor Master Benedick is a villain of grand proportions, but each is selfish and irresponsible, and each is punished justly. Jack, who twice faces the complications of wooing women in the story, pursues his goals responsibly, modestly, and honorably. His reward is love, respect, and wealth.

Another minor character whose personality is well defined is Mistress Franke, the old gossip who interferes in the domestic affairs of Jack and his second wife. Unlike Will Sommers, Benedick, and Sir George Rigley, who feel superior to the English merchants, Mistress Franke is trying to bring Mistress Winchcombe down to her level. By giving the young wife bad advice on how to run her household, the old woman creates a conflict between Jack and his wife. When Mistress Franke again visits the Winchcombe house while both Jack and his wife are absent, she shows an unwarranted disrespect for the famous clothier and his wife by telling the servants that Mistress Winchcombe is a "draggle tayle girle" and calling the master of the house "plaine Iacke." As in the case of Benedick and Sir George, the old woman is rewarded for her lack of courtesy when the servants of the house get her drunk and pay to have her hauled about the town in a basket to be displayed to her neighbors. The sight of the presumptuous old busybody being carried about in a basket because she is too drunk to walk or talk properly is a source of much laughter among her neighbors. The scene must also have struck the fancies of Deloney's readers, who would certainly have known Mistress Frankes in their own experiences. Thematically, Deloney shows the self-regulation and hence the continued vitality of a working society. Having established the right atmosphere of an orderly household, Jack and his wife can be absent and still expect order to be maintained by the servants, just as the enlightened King can expect Jack to discharge his responsibilities toward the commonwealth.

Such comic scenes as the one of Mistress Franke wagging her drunken head and asking, "Who co mee, who?" instead of "who knows me" and that of the profligate draper Randoll Pert, who, while attempting to escape someone who was not in fact chasing him, trips when his pants fall down, show Deloney's ability to use farce and pathos in the same scenes and make them both work.[44] Similarly, the scene in which Mistress Franke has been given too much to drink causes the reader to disdain her actions and at the same time to pity her insecurity:

I thanke God I am not drunke: Mistresse *Winchcombe*, mistresse? No, Nan *Winchcombe*, I will call her name, plaine *Nan*: what, I was a woman when she was sirreuerence a paltry gurle, though now shee goes in her Hood and Chaine of Gold: what care I for her?

(p. 62; sig. L2)

The theme of moderation is also present in the Mistress Franke episode. She is not an effective part of the industrious ant hill. Of Jack, the model, we are told, never "at any time would hee bee ouercome in drinke" (p. 3; sig. A2).

Deloney's characters are often at least partially defined by the language they use. Apart from brief lapses into euphuistic style in the speeches of Jack's first wife,[45] the characters in *Jack of Newbury* use

a variety of language that Deloney doubtless heard used by middle-
class merchants and their associates. Deloney flavors the dialogue of
the delightful parents of Jack's second wife with what is probably the
first use of dialect in English prose. In the manner of Gammer, Hodge,
Tib, and the other rustics in *Gammer Gurton's Needle,* Mistress
Winchcombe's father uses the coarse language and the malapropisms
of folks not acquainted with reading and the language of polite society:

Marry heare you (quoth the old man) I vaith cham but a poore man, but I
thong God, cham of good exclamation among my neighbours, and they will
as zoone take my vice for any thing as a richer mans: thicke I will bestow,
you shall haue with a good will, because che heare very good condemnation
of you in euery place, therefore chill giue you twenty Nobles and a weaning
Calfe, and when I dye and my wife, you shall haue the reuelation of all my
goods.

(p. 21; sig. D3)

Deloney's ear was also tuned to the use and misuse of English by
foreigners. Much of the trouble the Italian merchant Benedick finds
himself in is caused by the fact that "hee could speak but bad English"
(p. 47; sigs. H4–H4v). The fact that his dialect is more German than
Italian does not make him more easily understood by Joan. To her he
is merely foreign. He tries to woo Joan by offering her silk for a frock,
but what he says is, "First; me wil giue you de silke for make you a
Frog" (p. 47; sig. H4v). Second, he offers her materials for a ruff, and
third, materials for a handkerchief. But his third offer sounds wrong:
"The turd shall be for make fen handkercher, for wipe your nose" (p.
47; sig. H4v). When Joan replies that she does not intend to marry,
Benedick asks her merely to sit on his bed and let him kiss her, but
again his words do not convey his thoughts: "Oh tis no matter for mar-
rye, if you will come in my chamber, beshit my bed, and let mee kiss
you" (p. 48; sig. H4v). Joan wants to have nothing to do with the young
Italian because, as Deloney says, "She that could not well vnderstand
his broken language, mistooke his meaning in many things" (p. 48; sig.
H4v). Benedick would have been better off had he, like Owen Glen-
dower's daughter, spoken no English at all.

Most of the characters in *Jack of Newbury* speak what Ernest A.
Baker calls "Deloney's natural dialogue." Here, according to Baker, is
"the best dialogue that had been seen as yet in an English prose tale."[46]
The widow's repartee in answer to her suitors in Chapter I, for exam-

ple, rivals the courtly language of literary ladies for wit and pithiness, yet it is not overly ornamented. When both the tanner and the parson announce that they intend to marry her immediately, she responds:

Nay soft (said the Widow) one Swallow makes not a Summer, nor one meeting a marriage: as I lighted on you vnlookt for, so came I hither vnprouided for the purpose.

I trust (quoth the Tanner) you came not without your eyes to see, your tongue to speake, your eares to heare, your hands to feele, nor your legs to goe. I brought my eyes (quoth she) to discerne colours, my tongue to say No to questions I like not, my hands to thrust from mee the things that I loue not, my eares to iudge twixt flattery and friendship, and my feet to run from such as would wrong mee.

(p. 11; sig. B4)

In like manner, when the hero Jack speaks, it is always with clarity and care. Although he uses much allegory and allusion, Jack is nevertheless not pompous in his language. He speaks to king, queen, or nobleman with language in no way inferior to theirs, and the King and Queen reply to him as they would to any nobleman, as by his speech he appears to be. Jack is, as he knows, the king of clothiers. When Jack smears his face and clothes with blood and comes before the Queen, he explains his appearance thus:

May it please your Grace (quoth hee) to vnderstand, that it was my chance to meete with a monster, who like the people *Cynomolgy*, had the proportion of a man, but headed like a dogge, the biting of whose teeth was like the poisoned teeth of a Crocodile, his breath like the Basilisks, killing afarre off. I vnderstand, his name was Enuie, who assailed mee inuisibly, like the wicked spirit of *Mogunce*, who flung stones at men, and could not bee seene: and so I come by my scratcht face, not knowing when it was done.

(p. 24; sig. E1)

Such ill will on the part of the nobility toward the middle class was apparently not unusual during the Renaissance.[47] Jack is, nevertheless, at least the equal of gentlemen in actions and in learning, as the Queen recognizes. She remarks that he is "a Clothier by trade, yet a Gentleman by condition" (p. 24; sig. E1). Interestingly, Jack's greatest antagonist in the novel is Cardinal Wolsey, the Oxford-educated son of a butcher. Wolsey is the "Prince of Butterflies" against whom, among others, Jack is defending the ant hill in Chapter III.

Jack's special dislike for Wolsey is apparently caused not only by the fact that the Cardinal is helping to thwart trade, but also by the fact that he is a man of common birth who sacrifices the common good for his own advancement. A class-conscious man, Wolsey had turned his back upon the traditional economic system based in the community, and in so doing must have become the symbol for Deloney of the new acquisitiveness in English society which was causing the social and economic upheaval of the late sixteenth century. Jack chides Wolsey for delaying the decree that would bring relief to the economically depressed clothiers when he reminds the Cardinal that his own advancement was made possible by the industry of a common man:

Trust me . . . if my Lord Cardinalls father had been no hastier in killing of Calues, than hee is in dispatching of poor mens sutes, I doubt he had neuer worne a Myter.

(p. 45: sigs. H3–H3v)

Deloney describes Wolsey as having "a loftie aspiring mind" (p. 46; sig. H3v), whereas Jack, whose goal was always the welfare of England, refused the King's offer to make him a knight. Wolsey was also, of course, a Catholic who became an enemy of Henry VIII and so of Elizabeth.

Deloney often defines the characters in *Jack of Newbury* by comparing them to the weather, the elements, plants, and animals. There is more imagery in this novel than in any of Deloney's other works. Animal imagery is the most noticeable.[48] There are, for example, 187 references to seventy-seven different animals in this one work alone. The most elaborate image is the widow's allegorical dream in Chapter I, where she sees a dove that has been "dismaid" at the sight of a hog. When she picks up the dove, she finds she has in her hands her own heart pierced with an arrow. A woman crowned like a queen tells her that her heart will die unless she anoints it with hog grease. She returns home to find the hog "rustling among the Loomes" and then awakens from her dream, "Being all in a sweate and very ill" (p. 9; sig. B3). The widow is, clearly, the dove wounded with cupid's arrow, and Jack is the hog, low of birth but nevertheless a delicacy, whom she finds in her own workshop.[49]

In addition to using such imagery to help define characters, Deloney also uses animal lore to emphasize the didactic messages of history. Announcing in his dedication that no art is more beneficial to England than "the most necessary Art of Clothing" (p. 2; sig. A2), Deloney consistently reemphasizes his theme. He uses the lowly ant as an image when, as King Henry VIII passes near Newbury, Jack and his men arm themselves and stand guard around an ant hill near where the King must pass. Jack identifies himself to the King as the Prince of Ants and says that he and his men are guarding the industrious ants against the idle butterflies. The problem Deloney is emphasizing is political and economic in nature, and more than merely a complaint against the interference of government in private business. The ants are, of course, the industrious tradesmen who are the backbone of the traditional community-based economy of England; and the mole, grasshopper, and caterpillar are those lazy new Englishmen who live off the industry of others and destroy them. The chief butterfly is Cardinal Wolsey who, through taxes and trade restrictions designed to profit entrepreneurs, has so injured business that "the poore Ant could no sooner get an egg into her nest, but he would haue it away" (p. 28; sig. E4). To give the King a concrete symbol of the moral, Jack's wife presents the royal couple with a golden beehive depicting "The figure of a flourishing Commonwealth." Lady Prudence and noble Fortitude tread under their feet the serpents Ambition, Envy, and Treason, "which seeke the downfall of this fruitfull tree" (p. 29; sig. E4v). Similar allegories throughout the novel are used to describe political and economic ideas in a concrete manner.

Possibly Deloney's animal imagery reveals a pessimistic view of man and society. Certainly when a character is compared to a worm or dog, the implication is not flattering. Wolsey as a caterpillar or butterfly is not a man but a greedy insect. But when Jack is compared to a hog, the reference is not negative. Jack and his workers are not demeaned by being compared to ants and bees. The suggestion is not that they are less than human, but that they are industrious and productive. The hog, unflattering as the comparison seems, is not, like the caterpillar, a parasite. It is a useful part of the commonwealth. Deloney uses animal imagery because his audience is familiar with the traditional traits and characteristics awarded animals and insects, not because he sees man generally descending to the level of beasts.

The theme of *Jack of Newbury* is obviously utilitarian. But the characters, language, imagery, and anecdotes presented by Deloney create an interesting and surprisingly coherent story of English life in the small town of Newbury, of middle-class Renaissance life generally, and of the heroic John Winchcombe specifically. Jack is, like most of Delo-

ney's major characters, a "presider,"[50] and as such he is given none of
the identifying foibles of a Mistress Franke, or the later Tom Drum or
Anthony Now-now. But there is some complexity to his character.

To be sure, Jack is an idealized character. Merritt Lawlis oversim-
plifies when he declares that Jack is "allowed only a passive role in the
action of the story."[51] It is true that his passions, his flaws, and his psy-
chology are never explored; like the heroes of dramatic comedy, Jack
faces and overcomes conflicts; and the reader or audience is pleased
when all ends happily for him. On occasion Jack is more than a hero
of comedy, as when he takes arms on behalf of the industrious clothiers
against the power of the state. The same sense of pride, or more accurately a sense of enlightened self-interest, that led Deloney himself to
write the "Ballad on the Want of Corn," causes Jack to make his protest to King Henry VIII. When a messenger orders Jack into the pres-
ence of the King during the "ant hill" battle early in the work, Jack
refuses to move from his "post," pleading responsibility of rule. Here
Jack is more than mere "presider." The King disarms the situation by
bending, much to the relief of Jack's men, who "with a ioyfull cry
flung vp their caps in token of victory" (p. 28; sig. E3v).

Jack is thus seen not merely as a passive man who rules his industrial
empire. He is also a character who believes and strongly defends the
worth of any man who is honest and hardworking and thus defends
the orderly commonwealth. Deloney's own democratic ideas are
behind the character of Jack, for Deloney had also been arrested, along
with fourteen other English weavers, and sent to jail for complaining
about unfair trade practices. John Winchcombe is therefore interesting
for more than his role as the unifying character in *Jack of Newbury:*
he is a man of carefully defined principle, who is willing to risk his
own security to insure the health of the commonwealth and one created with a degree of autobiography.

III   Thomas of Reading

A   *The Sources*

The sources Deloney drew on for his story of the six worthy yeomen
of the west are, like those of *Jack of Newbury*, mainly folktales and
legends. But where Jack was without doubt an historical character, the
six worthy yeomen, including Thomas Cole, probably are not. In the
foreword to *Jack of Newbury* Deloney announced plans "to set to your

sight the long hidden History of *Thomas of Reading, George of Glocester, Richard of Worcester,* and *William of Salisbury,* with divers others" (p. 2; sig. A2v). By the time he got around to telling his story, the names of several of his characters had changed so that the name of the individual clothier alliterates with the name of his home: Gray of Gloucester, Sutton of Salisburie, William of Worcester, Simon of Southhampton, as well as Thomas Cole of Reading and Tom Dove of Exeter. In addition, Deloney includes three clothiers from the North: Cutbert of Kendall, Hodgekins of Halifax, and Martin Byram of Manchester.[52] All of the geographical areas described by Deloney were known as clothing centers, but there is no historical evidence that any of these heroes ever lived. Thomas Fuller, after sketching the life of the Thomas Cole he knew from "Tradition and an authorless pamphlet,"[53] recognizes that there is little fact on which to base the details of the story. Fuller dismisses the argument by saying, "However, because *omnis fabula fundatur Historia,* let this Cole be accounted eminent in this kind; though I vehemently suspect very little of truth would remain in the midst of the story, if the gross falsehoods were pared from both sides thereof."[54]

Still the setting of the novel is historical. The story of Henry I and his brother Robert is drawn from Holinshed (II, pp. 28–46);[55] but Deloney adds to the history a rather conventional romance between Duke Robert and Margaret, the beautiful daughter of the Earl of Shrewsbury, and three stories dealing with the several clothiers.

The story of a law of Halifax which allowed merchants to execute thieves in Halifax and which led finally to the invention and use of a guillotine also has its basis in Holinshed (I, p. 185) and other chronicles. Mann suggests that Deloney need not have relied upon Holinshed alone for the story, however, for the reputation of Halifax among traveling minstrels would have been well known.[56] As a part of this story Deloney uses the description in Holinshed (I, p. 209) of the Scottish hero William Wallace, whom Deloney calls Wallis. Another element Deloney uses, the device of having the horses' shoes nailed on backwards in order to deceive pursuers, comes from yet another Scottish hero—Robert the Bruce—who was well known from folktales and described by Holinshed (I, p. 213).

Deloney returns to the use of the *novella* for his story of Sir William Ferris's overlarge nose. The trick played on Calandrino in *The Decameron* (third story, ninth day) is of the same type as that played on Ferris. In Boccaccio's story the gullible Calandrino is persuaded by some comrades that he is pregnant. By pseudomedical treatment he is both relieved of some money and made "well." The use of the bladder-of-blood trick is a common device.[57] But perhaps the direct source for Deloney's episode of the nose is to be found in Reginald Scot's *Discoveries of Witchcraft*, published in 1584,[58] Scot tells the story of a man convinced that his nose is "as big as a house." When neither friend nor physician can persuade him that his nose is of normal size, a new physician is summoned, who empties stale blood, along with pieces of beef liver, into a tub while the patient is blindfolded. Upon seeing the corruption he supposes has been removed from his nose, the patient believes that his nose is now normal.

The central episode, that of the murder of Thomas Cole, almost certainly comes from tradition and may be based upon an actual murder or murders committed in Colnbrook, a small community between Reading and London. The present owner of the Ostrich Inn in Colnbrook will show visitors the room where Thomas Cole met his doom, and he will explain that the town got its name from the notoriety following the revelation that Cole was murdered there and his body thrown in the brook, thus Colebrooke or Colnbrook. Although the story of the murders committed at the Ostrich Inn (Deloney's Crane Inn) is well known to modern residents of Colnbrook, not even the present owner of the Ostrich Inn knew of Thomas Deloney.

What Deloney takes from legends, folktales, and chronicles is usually little more than an idea. Names and places are changed to fit his context, but the context itself appears to be Deloney's own invention. He had no need to borrow works or ideas from stories about clothiers, for he knew the language, habits, problems, hopes, and fears of clothiers from personal experience. The story of Sir William Ferris's nose is used as an ornament, a popular tale to decorate his story of the clothiers. There seems to be no political or social reason why he should have chosen that story rather than any other popular tale. When he writes about the King's kindness toward the clothiers of Halifax, he borrows two authentic thieves and an account of the invention of the guillotine from history, uses the parts he wants, and discards the rest. William Wallace and Robert the Bruce are not important as individuals in the story. Deloney needed thieves in his tale so that he could make a point about the importance of the clothing industry to the economy of England; Wallace and Bruce were major figures in British history and therefore useful to Deloney.

B *The Plot*

King Henry I, who had seized the crown of England while his brother Robert was out of the country, is forced to wait beside the road while over two hundred carts loaded with cloth pass. He learns that the carts belong to Thomas Cole, and later when he meets more wagons taking cloth to London, he realizes that England's strength lies in her clothing industry. In London Thomas Cole and several other clothiers gather to eat and play games after they finish their business.

In the meantime, Margaret, daughter of the banished Earl of Shrewsbury, has been "quite turned out of doors succorlesse and friendlesse." She joins some maidens going to the Gloucestershire Fair to seek employment and is able to find a job as a servant for the wife of Gray of Gloucester. First Gray and then his wife want to dismiss Margaret because her beauty is distracting to the weavers and to Gray, but Margaret's lament changes their minds.

King Henry invites England's chief clothiers to London, seeking to strengthen the main business of England. The clothiers ask that cloth measures be standardized, that broken coins be made legal tender, and that permission be granted to hang the thieves who plague the clothiers of Halifax. The King grants all these requests.

In order to show their gratitude to the King, the clothiers plan a party for his two sons. Cutbert of Kendall dallies with the young wife of the innkeeper of Bosom's Inn, is caught, and is tied up in the smokehouse. When the princes finish their banquet, the clothiers ask that they come to the aid of Cutbert; at the request of the princes, Old Bosom releases him.

The wife of Simon of Southhampton badgers her husband to take her to London. Pleading that he must attend to business, he agrees to let her go without him. Accompanied by a male servant, she meets the wives of Gray, Fitzallen, and Cole on a journey to London, where they visit all the tourist sites and observe London fashions. Upon her return home, Simon's wife begins to press for fine clothes. When her husband argues that country women do not need such expensive gowns, she apparently falls into a swoon. When she gets her gown, she recovers immediately.

With the help of the clothiers, King Henry defeats France and makes a prisoner of his brother Robert. Allowed to hunt and hawk over the countryside, Robert meets Margaret and falls in love with her. The courtship continues secretly while the clothiers honor King Henry with parties, gifts, and pledges of loyalty.

The new law in Halifax which allows thieves to be hanged discourages thievery until "Mighty Wallis," a famous thief, decides to venture his neck for some Northern cloth. Although Wallis and his men escape capture for some time by nailing their horses' shoes on backward, they are at last captured and sentenced to die. No one, however, will agree to act as hangman, and the thieves leave town. Hodgekins gets permission from the King to use a machine that will sever a man's head without the aid of an executioner, and thereafter Halifax uses the guillotine to rid their area of thieves.

Duke Robert continues to woo Margaret and persuades her to marry him secretly. Sir William Ferris, a married man, courts Margaret also. To get rid of him, she says that she cannot love him because he has an "ill-favoured great nose," whereupon Ferris falls into a deep melancholy. His wife finally persuades a cunning physician to seem to remove "foul blood" from the knight's nose to return it to normal size. The physician empties a bladder of sheep's blood into a basin and makes Ferris believe that his nose is now normal.

During this same time Thomas Cole is marked for murder and robbery by the Jarmons, innkeepers of the Crane Inn at Colebrooke, where Cole often stops on trips to and from London. After four fortuitous escapes, Cole's luck deserts him. Assigned to a room that has a special bed, Cole is melancholy and falls into a fitful sleep. The Jarmons tilt the special bed, allowing Cole to slide through a trap door into a boiling caldron in the kitchen below. He is robbed and his body thrown into the river. Because Cole's horse breaks free, Jarmon's story that Cole had ridden off before daybreak is disproved. Both Jarmon and his wife are hanged.

One day after the murder of Cole the clothiers' wives come to Salisbury to attend a churching feast in honor of Sutton's new son. A great deal of misinformation about the murder is passed around, including the idea that Cole's horse spoke and revealed the murder. Sutton, however, lays the rumors to rest.

Duke Robert eludes his guards and meets Margaret in the forest. His guards pursue, capture both lovers, and put them in prison. The King agrees to release Margaret but stipulates that she must witness the blinding of Robert. Margaret decides to give all her earthly goods to the poor and to spend the rest of her life in a convent. The King praises her decision.

Thomas Dove falls into debt and is deserted by all his servants. He is arrested in London but escapes with the aid of the giant innkeeper at Jarrat's Hall. One of his servants, however, betrays Dove to an officer of the law, and Dove is arrested. As he is being led to prison, a messenger carrying Thomas Cole's will arrives. Dove is given money willed him by his friend Cole, and the other clothiers contribute to help him start life anew. He works hard and redeems himself, paying his creditors and living out his life in great wealth.

C Analysis

Deloney's primary purpose in *Thomas of Reading* is once again to praise the clothing industry and to show its importance to the prosperity and general well-being of England. In the introduction to the novel, Deloney calls the clothing industry the "onely chiefe" craft and says that "the one halfe of the people in the land liued in those daies thereby" (p. 213; sig. A2). Chapter I sets the theme which Deloney follows throughout the work. King Henry I must stand to the side of the road while Thomas Cole's wagons go by carrying cloth to London. Initially angered, as we might expect he would be, Henry quickly realizes that since the wealth of England depends upon the clothiers, he needs to encourage them. His actions throughout the rest of the novel show that he sees his responsibility as King is to aid the clothing industry in every way he can. Further, Henry recognizes that he is not England, but the servant of England. England is "a fertile Countrie and faithfull subiects," and "it would neuer grieue a King to die for the defence" of his country (p. 215, sig. A3v). Later, the King clearly outlines his role vis-à-vis the commonwealth:

The strength of a King is the loue and friendship of his people, and he gouernes ouer his Realme most surely, that ruleth iustice with mercy: for he ought to feare many, whom many do feare: therefore the gouernors of the Common-wealth ought to observe two speciall precepts: the one is, that they so maintain the profit of the Commons, that whatsoeuer in their calling they doe, they referre it therevnto: the other, that they be alwaies as well carefull ouer the whole Common-wealth, as ouer any part thereof; lest while they vphold the one, the other be brought to vtter decay.

(p. 226; sig. C2)

As long as the model operates according to those principles in all of its parts, life is good, people (from monarch to peasant) are happy, and everyone is prosperous. The King governs not so much by divine right as by the will of the governed. In *Thomas of Reading*, for example, Duke Robert has the greater claim to the throne under the medieval doctrine of divine right, but Henry has the support of the people. Deloney thus constructs a more democratic concept of divine right. When the commonwealth reflects the divinely ordered cosmos, as that order was viewed by the Protestant of Elizabethan England, it works to the benefit of all. The concept of a divinely planted king was surely too close to the Catholic model of divinely appointed Pope to appeal to the staunchly Protestant Deloney. Deloney's Henry I, like his Henry VIII in *Jack of Newbury*, is King because his qualities enable him to rule effectively.

The commonwealth model of rule extends to all segments of government. The effective businessmen are those who, like the effective king, recognize their responsibilities both to the state and to society. The effective journeymen are those who respect their good masters and the roles of the apprentices under them. The model applies to husbands, wives, servants, innkeepers—in short, to all in the commonwealth. The various classes are separate in the sense that their duties are different, but they are of equal importance in the commonwealth.

Thomas of Reading is probably the best constructed of all Deloney's novels. True, it is episodic, as the others are, but here Deloney juggles several related plots, and he ends the work without leaving anything unresolved. The novel is not about Thomas Cole any more than *Jack of Newbury* is about John Winchcombe. Neither is it about the six worthy yeomen of the West who are mentioned in the subtitle nor the nine clothiers whose lives are discussed in the work. Rather, the novel is about the honor, dignity, and economic worth of middle-class merchants in England and their place in the English commonwealth. The various episodes, including the subplot of Margaret and Duke Robert, are all relevant to Deloney's central theme because they are all attached to the actions of the clothiers.

The major characters in *Thomas of Reading* are portrayed idealistically, but they are not romantic characters out of a fairy tale. Thomas Cole and his fellow clothiers are hard-working, intelligent, productive merchants who deal with everyday problems. Gray of Gloucester worries that his wife's new maid will distract his workers with her beauty, and his wife worries that the same beauty will turn her husband's head. Simon of Southhampton is concerned that his wife's desire for fine clothes will reflect badly upon his reputation, but his love for her overrides his concern for social propriety.[59] Hodgekins, though he knows he must protect his property, cannot bring himself personally to hang a thief. To be sure, the various episodes of the novel are closer to romance than to reality, but the complications are of middle-class life of any age, not of chivalric romance.

The characters in *Thomas of Reading,* moreover, are individuals. Tom Dove likes large parties with much music and many women, Cutbert prefers smaller and more intimate liaisons, and Simon neglects everything for a mess of pottage. Thomas Cole's personality is less flamboyant than most of the others', but he does display a sharp wit, a strong affection for his family and friends, and a love of gambling. Among the women, Margaret is the most remarkable character. Her speech, her ideas, and her every action show her to be a young lady of intellect and education, but still very young. Her mistress, Mrs. Gray, is a woman of kindness and devotion, who, unlike the friends of Tom Dove, does not desert those she loves in difficult times. Even the women at Mrs. Sutton's churching feast, who might be thought of as sterotypically ignorant, gabbing women (Deloney uses an old proverb to describe the scene involving the women: "Many women many words"), are not all of a kind. Mrs. Gray is willing to believe the story of Cole's horse speaking, and another uses the biblical story of Balaam's ass to support the idea. A third woman, however, bluntly labels such outlandish ideas as lies, and a fourth woman compromisingly suggests that while it is possible that the horse might have spoken, the story is unlikely.

The episode involving Margaret and Duke Robert seems almost alien to the rest of the novel. The young people of noble birth are characters out of a romance, and in the hands of John Lyly or Thomas Lodge they would surely have been given a happier existence. In Deloney's story, the noble Robert is blinded and the beautiful Margaret enters a convent. Further, implicit in the episode is the question of usurpation.

Deloney's characters do not discuss the justness of Henry's claim to the throne or the rightness of his actions. They do support Henry I in his fight against Robert just as Jack of Newbury supported Henry VIII in his wars with James. Deloney tells us that when Henry I requested troops be sent from England to aid him in France "the Clothiers at their owne proper cost set out a great number, and set them ouer to the King" (p. 240; sig. E3). Henry had made great efforts to solidify the commonwealth against the threat of disorder by doing everything possible "to winne the good will of his Nobilitie, and to get the fauor of the Commons by curtesie: for the obtaining whereof hee did them many fauours" (p. 214; sigs. A2v-A3). Deloney therefore avoids confronting the issue of usurpation by having his middle-class workers defend the King, who clearly had their best interests in mind. Technically no usurpation takes place because Robert is never King. Henry is King, a good ruler; and his subjects, loyal to the concept of an orderly commonwealth, support him.

The curious fall of Robert and Margaret may be seen, therefore, as justly deserved; for both violate the King's orders instead of being loyal subjects. Romantic they are, but foolish and dangerous to the peace and order of the realm. By tying herself to Robert, Margaret aligns herself with someone who is in opposition to the King, the same position she had found herself in when her father, the Earl of Shrewsbury, had opposed the King. Being a part of a family who did not have the well-being of the commonwealth at heart, Margaret is "quite turned out of doores succorlesse and friendlesse" (p. 216, sig. A4). She found a comfortable, secure life among the clothiers, but she left that life to marry Robert, another man who sought to bring chaos into the ordered commonwealth. For punishment, Robert is blinded and Margaret enters a convent where she will be permanently and irrevocably a part of an enduring society.

Robert and Margaret are, therefore, examples of wrong action in the commonwealth, albeit their errors are understandable and relatively minor. Cutbert of Kendall and Old Bosom's wife are likewise discordant elements in society. Their liaison endangers the family unit, the microcosm of the commonwealth and of the cosmos. Cutbert is punished by being hanged up in the rafters of a smokehouse, but because he is a member of the respected class of clothiers and because he is "greatly ashamed" (p. 233; sig. D2), he is released by the Prince, Henry's son. The seriousness of the transgression is not lightened by the burlesque nature of it, however. The Prince tells Bosom, "if euer hereafter you catch him in the corne, clappe him in the pownd" (p. 233; sigs. D2-D2v)

A more serious example of violation of the commonwealth ideal is found in the episode involving the Jarmons, hosts of the Crane Inn. Instead of protecting their guests, as in an orderly society, the greedy Jarmons sacrifice propriety for money. The same type of acquisitiveness Deloney wrote about in *Canaans Calamitie*, the violation of social law which brought God's wrath upon Jerusalem, is therefore present in Colnbrooke, England, at the Crane Inn. The desire for profit unaccompanied by primary responsibility to society is here presented as so injurious to the commonwealth that it destroys its most productive citizen, Thomas Cole.

The story of the innkeepers in Colnbrooke was surely known throughout southern England in Deloney's day as it is today. The inclusion of a popular legend thus lends an immediacy, a reality, to Deloney's work. No doubt we see the characters in *Thomas of Reading* as Deloney and his readers saw them. The women chatting at the churching feast present a realistic picture of what Deloney must have observed many times; for here are women, ordinarily isolated, now able to meet and talk with their own kind. They are for the reader both amusing and delightful. They get along well with each other, as purposeful people usually do; they can joke with serving men in a slightly risqué manner without losing their essential dignity; and they are sincerely concerned to learn of the beastly murder of a good man. Tom Dove, Simon, Cutbert, Old Bosom, and even Jarmon are characters whose traits particularize them without making them mere caricatures. Like Dickens's Mr. Micawber in *David Copperfield*, Deloney's characters are two-dimensional, emblematic composites of types of people Deloney must have known.

The language of the characters in *Thomas of Reading* is as individual as their personalities. Hodgekins, a "rough-hewn fellow" from northern England, shows that Deloney's ear for dialect was not restricted to the dialect of Buckinghamshire, where the parents of John Winchcombe's wife lived. Addressing the King, Hodgekins says,

Yea, gude faith, mai Liedge, the faule eule of mai saule, giff any thing will keepe them whiat, till the karles be hanged by the cragge. What the dule care they for boaring their eyne, sea lang as they mae gae groping vp and downe the Country like fause lizar lownes, begging and craking?

(p. 227; sig. C3)

The King finds Hodgekins's "broad Northerne speech" entertaining, but he speaks plain, idiomatic English himself. He answers Hodgekins:

I think it not amisse to ordain this death for such malefactors: and peculiarly to the towne of *Hallifax* I give this priuiledge, That whosoeuer they finde stealing their Cloth, being taken with the goods, that without further iudgment, they shall be hanged vp.

(p. 227: sig. C3)

Thomas Cole's language is in no way inferior to that of the King. A man of quality and responsibility himself, his dialogue is every bit as clear, specific, and concise as the King's. Suggesting that the clothiers host a banquet for the King's sons, he says,

> ... we will prepare a banquet for them at our hoast Garrats, who as you know, hath a faire house, and goodly roomes: Besides, the man himselfe is a most couragious mind and good behauiour, sufficient to entertain a Prince: his wife also is a daunty fine Cooke: all which considered, I know not a fitter place in *London*.
>
> (p. 228; sig. C3v)

Coles's language is the language Deloney uses when he narrates his stories. It is the simple, clear, expressive language of the educated tradesman of the Renaissance, who showed, according to Louis B. Wright, "a developing language consciousness" that was "evident even among the less erudite middle class."[60] And it is while writing the language he knows best that Deloney creates his most memorable characters and tells his most interesting stories.

If he is at his best writing idiomatic English, Deloney is no less at home with the rougher talk of those citizens of coarser tongue. Bosom's wife is a wanton who can be clever in her speech, as when she observes Cutbert's advances and wants to signal him that she is, while not forward, yet certainly available. When Cutbert calls her "good wife," she replies that she is not necessarily good and he should call her "Mistress" (p. 219; sig. B1v). But while capable of using respectable language, she has obviously had enough experience in the back alley to pick up some of its language. In a mock argument with Cutbert, she shouts at him, "Why you gag-tooth iacke, you blinking companion, get thee out of my kitchen quickly, or with my powdered beefe broth, I will make your pate as bald as a friers" (p. 231; sig. D1).

This is the street language of Elizabeth Tudor's England, and it was newly portrayed in prose fiction by Deloney. Perhaps it is because the euphuistic tradition was so strong in the literature of his time and Deloney felt he had to prove he could use elevated language in the manner of Lyly and Greene that he inserts interludes of euphuism, what Ole Reuter calls "euphuistic excursions,"[61] into his novels. The episode of Margaret and Duke Robert illustrates the fact that members of noble families often turned to respected trades to earn a living and that violations of the commonwealth ideal would be punished. But in the speeches of the romantic characters Margaret and Robert the life almost leaves Deloney's novel. Margaret, in protesting Robert's proposal, uses classical allusions, intricate analogies with natural history, parallelism and antithesis in syntactic structure, assonance and alliteration in sound patterns, and all the other trappings of euphuism:

> ... far vnfit it is that the Turtle should match with the Eagle, though her loue be neuer so pure, her wings are vnfit to mount so high. While *Thales* gazed on the starres, he stumbled in a pit. And they that clime vnaduisedly, catch a fall suddenly: what auaileth high dignitie in time of aduersity?
>
> (p. 250; sig. G1)

And so on for many more lines. The improbable story of the two noble lovers whose lives end in sorrow has probably attracted many readers and not a few tears over the years, but the language used in Margaret's and Robert's dialogue is stilted and clearly out of place in the world of simple prose.

Noticeably lacking in *Thomas of Reading* is the elaborate use of imagery that is found in *Jack of Newbury* and the two novels dealing with the shoemakers. Deloney writes that musicians follow Tom Dove "as little chickens after a hen," and the episodes with Margaret and Duke Robert have elaborate images common to euphuism. But in this novel there is not the profusion of imagery awarded the middle-class characters in Deloney's other novels. It is tempting to believe that Deloney did not want to dilute the romantic episodes by sprinkling imagery throughout the novel.

The most remarkable element in *Thomas of Reading,* and in the other novels as well, is not Deloney's experimentations with various prose styles, but his attention to detail in individual scenes. His development of appropriate setting, characterization, and unity within episodes is what one might expect from a competent writer. But there are occasional examples of superior artistic talent to be found in Deloney's works. From the point of view of both craftsmanship and psychological insight, the episode of Thomas Cole's murder and the comic scene that follows illustrate the height of Deloney's artistic ability. He creates dramatic tension with Cole's fortuitous escapes from death, and he further establishes the significance of the action by expanding it beyond the realm of bestial murder to a level of cosmic importance. Besides the forebodings the good man Cole has that he will die, the action takes place at night and is accompanied by the indignant shrieks of nature, specifically of the owl and the raven. This use of cosmic signs as a means of setting the mood, instead of the use of careful character motivation, indicates a certain naiveté in Deloney. Shakespeare carefully establishes the strengths and weaknesses of his characters in *Macbeth*, has Macbeth and Lady Macbeth make their decisions, and then uses cosmic signs to magnify emotionally the horror of their actions. Shakespeare thus creates both an emotional and an intellectual impact upon his audience, whereas Deloney is able to attain only the emotional impact. The point is, however, that while the scene does not measure up to the work of Shakespeare, it is nevertheless an effective scene.

The scene of murder, certainly the focal point of the novel, is followed by a comic scene. This dramatic device, which accentuates the horror of the murder while at the same time keeping it from immobilizing all further action, is so similar to the scene of the drunken porter in *Macbeth* that one almost certainly influenced the other.[62] In Chapter XII, where Deloney presents a churching feast, the clothiers' wives gather to celebrate the birth of a son to Sutton's wife. The women gossip about their husbands, their servants, and their neighbors. They enter into witty dialogue with the serving men, Crab, Weasel, and Wren. The conversation is full of inconsequential talk of women's clothes, fleas, and buttocks.

In the midst of friendly chatter, the murder of Cole is brought up, and each woman reports what she has heard of the terrible event. So laced with misinformation and supernatural explanations is the discussion, however, that the realistic horror of the murder is emphasized by the continuation of everyday life among the clothiers. The murder of the chief clothier of the land and the friend of the other major characters in the novel has had a strong impact upon the clothiers, but life must go on, and it does. When in Chapter XIII Deloney returns to the romantic story of Margaret and Duke Robert, it therefore is not out of place. Such appropriate focus and timing cause most scholars to recognize that *Thomas of Reading* is "notably superior in construction" to the other novels.[63]

IV   The Gentle Craft, Part 1

A   *The Sources*

When Deloney, in his note to "all courteous Readers" prefacing *The Gentle Craft, Part 1*, admonishes his readers to "read nothing except you read it all" (p. 72; sig. A2v), he does not mean that his novel builds carefully to a surprise conclusion, in the manner of a detective novel. When he says, "the beginning shews not the middle, and the middle shews not the latter end" (p. 72; sig. A2v), he means that there are three separate stories connected only by the fact that all three concern shoemakers. The first story presents the "history" of St. Hugh and St. Winifred and the origin of calling shoemakers' tools "St. Hugh's bones," thus giving the craft the status of legend; the second deals with the noble brothers Crispine and Crispianus, who become shoemakers, thus tying the craft historically to nobility; and the third tells how the shoemaker Simon Eyre becomes Lord Mayor of London, thus giving the craft social and political status.

As is usual with Deloney, many details in his stories come from tradition, but the main characters and the outlines of their adventures come from Caxton, Stow, and other writers. The St. Hugh-St. Winifred episode is a blending of stories from William Caxton's *Golden Legend*. Caxton tells of St. Ursula, the daughter of the British Christian King Notus or Maurus, whose hand is sought by the pagan son of an English king. Ursula, devout in her Christian faith and reluctant to marry a non-Christian, persuades her father to delay her marriage for three years, during which time the young man is to be baptized and instructed in the Christian faith. Ursula's plan is to discourage the young man's love, but he gladly accepts her conditions and does all that she asks.[64]

The story of St. Winifred, also from Caxton, tells of the Christian maid "so inflamed with . . . holy doctrine that she purposed to forsake all worldly pleasauncies and to serve Almighty God in meekness and chastity."[65] One Sunday while all other members of her household are at church and Winifred is at home ill, a young man comes to her home "for to defoul her." What he actually does is cut off her head. Caxton reports that on the spot where her head fell sprang up a fountain of clear water with healing qualities. In the blood-splattered rocks around the fountain, Caxton says, grew a soft, fragrant moss, "that endureth into this day."[66]

There is no Sir Hugh in the *Golden Legend;* Caxton's "Life of St. Ursula" and "Life of St. Winifred" tell the brief stories of virtuous women. We know that Caxton's Ursula was "divinely inspired" and his Winifred was "inflamed with . . . holy doctirne." But we know little else about the women and even less about the other characters. Deloney blends the two women into one character, introduces Sir Hugh in the place of Caxton's pagan son of the British king, and gives the characters thoughts and voices.

The origin of Sir Hugh and his connection with the shoemakers is unclear; perhaps Deloney's story is the origin, for M. P. Tilley lists Dekker's *Shoemakers' Holiday* (1601) as the first published reference to "St. Hugh's Bones,"[67] and Deloney's work, of course, predates Dekker's play. But since the story of a love-sick knight trying to win the favor of a lady is rather common in sixteenth-century romances, Deloney would not have had to look far to find what Mann calls "the conventional doings of the knight of romance."[68] What Deloney wants to do in this first episode is to spin a tale of romance that will be attractive to his readers and then to tie the hero and heroine to the shoemaking trade. The stories he takes from Caxton and expands upon are the "many matters of Delight, very pleasant to be read" he advertises on his title page, but his major purpose is to show his readers "what famous men have been Shoomakers in time past in this Land, with their worthy deeds and great Hospitality" (p. 69; sig. A1).

The Crispine-Crispianus story is also from Caxton. Persecuted for their Christian faith, Caxton's characters come to the city of Soissons in disguise to earn their living by working with their hands, thus following in "the steps of St. Paul, the apostle."[69] Mann thinks that the account of the French-British wars was suggested to Deloney by Grafton's *Chronicle*.[70] And almost certainly the story of Pyramus and Thisbe and of Romeo and Juliet influenced Deloney, for he adds to Caxton's story the star-crossed lovers Ursula and Crispine. Not only do the young lovers decide to marry despite warring families, but they also have a kindly friar to perform the marriage.

The story of Simon Eyre has its basis in John Stow's *Survey of London*. The details of Eyre's rise to high position, his contributions to buildings in London, and his charitable donations are all recorded by Stow. But the character of Eyre and his remarkable wife come either from tradition or from Deloney's imagination or, probably, from both. The details of workshop routine and chatter come from one who had sat at the workbench with his fellows.

B *The Plot*

In the first episode, Sir Hugh, son of the King of Powes, falls in love with the fair virgin Winifred, daughter of Donwallo, King of Tegina. Winifred, a new convert to Christianity, spurns Sir Hugh's love and asks him to absent himself so that she might "consider on this matter." After a three-month rustication, Sir Hugh returns to find that the meditative Winifred has quite forgotten him. Despondent, he leaves England to find a place where there are no women. He visits France and Italy, and after being shipwrecked he is cast up on the shore of Sicily, where he is confronted with the fabled Cyclops, wild lions, bears, bulls, dragons, elephants, and "many thousand more of other dangerous and cruell, ravenous Beasts." Finally escaping, he returns to England and works for a year among the jolly shoemakers.

At the end of his year with the shoemakers, Sir Hugh returns to Flentshire to renew his suit for Winifred. When he learns that she has been sentenced to die by the tyrant Dioclesian for refusing to yield to pagan law, Sir Hugh defends her faith and constancy so loudly that he too is arrested and sentenced to die. Winifred, seeing Sir Hugh's willingness to die for principle, pledges herself to him. Both are executed, and Sir Hugh leaves his bones, all he has, to his friends, the shoemakers, who carve the tools of their trade out of them, hence calling them "St. Hugh's bones."

In the second episode the Roman Emperor Maximinus cruelly seeks to imprison all the young men of noble birth in England. The Queen of Logria instructs her sons, Crispine and Crispianus, to disguise themselves as commoners and to seek a trade to support themselves. As the young men wander about the streets of Feversham, they hear a company of shoemakers singing at their work and decide to seek employment with them.

Crispine becomes shoemaker for the daughter of the Roman Emperor, Ursula, who falls in love with Crispine. They make plans to marry secretly, and Crispine seeks out a blind friar to perform the ceremony. After they are married, the young lovers spend the night in the Emperor's park, and at dawn Crispine accompanies Ursula to the palace and then returns to his master's shop.

During the same night Crispianus is conscripted into military service and sent to France to fight against the Persians. Crispianus distinguishes himself in battle and is sent home to be honored by Maximinus. The Emperor praises Crispianus and makes him second only to himself in authority. He wishes he could give the shoemaker the hand of his daughter in marriage, but she has disappeared.

Ursula, discovering herself pregnant, fled the palace and is living in the house of Crispine's master. After the birth of the child, Crispine brings Ursula to court where she is welcomed by her grateful father.

Maximinus tries to present Ursula's hand to Crispianus, but she insists that Crispine better deserves her love. When he learns that the shoemaker Crispine is brother to the valiant Crispianus, the Emperor blesses the wedding. The shoemakers in London rejoice and declare a holiday to celebrate the good fortune of their fellow craftsman.

The third episode introduces Simon Eyre, a London shoemaker who is industrious and respected. Eyre sees an opportunity to make a great deal of money when he learns that a Greek merchant ship laden with rich cloth has been driven ashore off the English coast. For an investment of £3,000, Eyre could make a substantial profit, but he has too little money. His wife persuades him to disguise himself as a rich Alderman and buy the cargo on credit, and Eyre is able to become rich by selling the valuable material for more than he paid for it. Recognized as a successful businessman, Eyre and his wife are invited to dinner by the Lord Mayor.

John the Frenchman and Haunce the Dutchman, shoemakers in Eyre's shop, are both in love with Florence, a serving girl. Haunce is able to interfere and lie enough to cause Florence and John to mistrust and finally dislike each other. John retaliates by upsetting the Dutchman's plans to meet privately with Florence. When she agrees to marry Haunce, John and Nick, an English journeyman in the house, invite Haunce to drink wine at a tavern on the night he is to be married. When Haunce passes out from drink, Nick slips away to try to persuade Florence to marry him. John tells a constable that Nick has murdered a man and is hiding at the abbey. Nick is arrested and John is able to meet Florence to renew his suit to her. But while he is speaking to her, a woman who had just arrived in England hears his voice and recognizes him as her husband. Florence, angry with foreigners, rejects Haunce and, on Eyre's advice, marries Nick.

Simon Eyre is chosen Sheriff of London, but he tells the Lord Mayor and the Alderman that his wealth and abilities are not great enough. The Lord Mayor hears that Eyre has a "little table" where he breakfasts which he will not sell for a thousand pounds. When the Lord Mayor offers to buy the table in exchange for all the wine Eyre will need in a year, Eyre accepts the position of Sheriff. He demonstrates the "little table" to the Alderman by having his wife lay a napkin on her lap and set a plate of venison on it.

When Eyre later is chosen Lord Mayor of London, he remembers a promise he had made when he was an apprentice, that when he became Mayor he would bestow a breakfast upon all apprentices in

London. He asks the Aldermen to declare a holiday on Shrove Tuesday and invite all the apprentices to his home for breakfast. Eyre lives out his life using his wealth to make life better in his community.

C Analysis

In *The Gentle Craft* Deloney continues to develop his theme of the successful middle-class merchant. But here, for the first time, he ventures outside his own specialty, the clothing industry, and tells the stories of "famous men [who] have been shoemakers in times past in the Land, with their worthy deeds and great Hospitality" (p. 69; sig. A1). Furthermore, the two parts of *The Gentle Craft* depart from Deloney's pattern of including an economic appeal for his heroes, as he did in both *Jack of Newbury* and *Thomas of Reading*. His purpose in *The Gentle Craft* is simply to show that shoemakers are and always have been good and noble members of society. If Deloney's shoemakers are not actually princes or knights who take up the trade, and they often are, they achieve nobility by their own efforts, as Simon Eyre does. An oft-repeated refrain in Part 1 of *The Gentle Craft* is "a shoomaker's son is a Prince born."

If Deloney's purpose in writing *The Gentle Craft, Part 1* is the same as his purpose in writing the other novels—to extol the economic, religious, and social benefits of middle-class merchants to England—his methods change somewhat with this work. In his earlier novels Deloney's emphasis was upon stories dealing with the working man. In *Thomas of Reading* we find several chapters dealing with Margaret and Duke Robert, but that venture into courtly romance is a minor subplot inserted into stories of the clothiers. Of the three major episodes in *The Gentle Craft, Part 1*, however, the first two concern the tribulations of the nobility. Written in a romantic manner fashionable to the age, the episode of St. Hugh in particular departs in large measure from Deloney's usual realistic scenes; he presents Sir Hugh in situations ranging from improbable to absurd. For example, at the point when he has been chased up a tree by wild beasts in the forests of Sicily, Sir Hugh sees a battle between an elephant and a dragon in which the dragon thrusts his head up the elephant's trunk and sucks the elephant's blood.[71] The elephant grows weak and falls dead upon the dragon, bursting the dragon into pieces. The episode of Crispine and Crispianus begins in the same romantic mood. Fortunately, Deloney quickly places the two young princes in a shoemaker's workshop rather than among the Cyclops, dragons, and stiff-jointed elephants, and the two young men become more shoemakers than romantic wanderers. It is not until the third episode that Deloney returns fully to the settings and characters he is best able to describe.

The progressive diminution of elements of romance in *The Gentle Craft, Part 1* mirrors the decline of aristocratic prestige and power during the late sixteenth century in England. Sir Hugh is a wanderer who is happy only when he is among the shoemakers. He speaks out in defense of Winifred, but he lacks political power to effect any change in the situation; indeed he succeeds only in involving himself in her problem and securing his own execution. While Sir Hugh's style of living and moral standards do not reflect those of many sixteenth-century noblemen, his lack of power does parallel the general deterioration of aristocratic political authority during Deloney's time. In like manner, the insecurity of the aristocratic class during the sixteenth century is represented by Crispine and Crispianus having to hide their identities to escape imprisonment. They are able to prosper only as shoemakers.[72]

But more important to Deloney's desire to emphasize the essential dignity of the middle-class worker is the fact that his first two episodes establish legendary and historical ties between shoemakers and the nobility. The St. Hugh legend gives the shoemakers a noble patron saint, thus cementing the craft securely in the holy order of things. The Crispine-Crispianus episode makes two princes the fellows of worthy shoemakers. Deloney lends dignity to the craft and firmly places it in the ranks of important elements in the commonwealth and, since St. Hugh was a shoemaker, in the cosmic order. In a time when such dramatists as Ben Jonson, especially in *The Alchemist* and *Volpone,* and Beaumont and Fletcher, especially in *The Knight of the Burning Pestle,* were portraying middle-class merchants as petty, avaricious, and bumbling, Deloney creates a context for his workers that is infinitely more flattering. His shoemakers are generous, responsible, kind, and occasionally even noble and saintly.

In the episode dealing with Simon Eyre Deloney presents busy, productive, happy characters. In the daily lives of these workers there is none of the political intrigue, isolation, or courtly problems found in the previous two episodes. Simon Eyre and his people have a good life, and their work is beneficial to their community and to England. Eyre, it is true, seeks to rise in fortune and reputation by capitalistic enterprise. Such were the opportunities offered by the commonwealth model constructed by Deloney, that the industrious craftsman can profit from his shrewd business practices and at the same time support society generally. In his success Eyre never rises so high as to cut ties with his foundation—the shoemaking trade. His duties as Lord Mayor are different from what they had been as apprentice shoemaker, but he is still a contributing part of the commonwealth. He uses his fortune and reputation to support the community economy. After he has given a party to honor the apprentice shoemakers of London, the Lord Mayor Eyre

builded *Leaden-Hall,* appointing that in the midst thereof, there should be a Market place kept euery Munday for Leather, where the Shoomakers of London, for their more ease, might buy of the Tanners without seeking any further.

(p. 133; sig. I4)

The romantic elements in *The Gentle Craft, Part 1* are far from Deloney's usual realistic detail, and inferior to it. The characters who appear in these romances are likewise generally less interesting than his hard-working craftsmen. So far are the details of the leisurely romances from Deloney's own experience that he often overlooks them. Sir Hugh's brother, for example, knows that Sir Hugh is forbidden to come near Winifred for three months, even though he is never informed of that fact. Deloney occasionally confuses details, too. In his rush to load the episode with courtly tradition, he has Sir Hugh refer to Winifred in particular and women in general as "vnconstant women, wauering and vncertain." There is much to complain of in Winifred's character, but inconstancy is not one of her flaws. Sir Hugh, and Deloney, is merely mouthing words without much concern for their relationship to fact.[73]

While Deloney's characters generally are superficial relative to characters in the best drama of the period, most of them have some trait to identify and particularize them. Yet Winifred remains a totally lifeless character throughout the episode. Although she is the stereotypically aloof woman of the courtly love tradition, we know less about her than we should. She is at first cruel to Sir Hugh, but she seems to have little reason to be so. After interrupting his suit to her for three months in order to please her, Sir Hugh returns to find that in her devotions to God she has forgotten all about him. Deloney does not analyze the obviously hypocritical position she illustrates when she, on the one hand, devotes herself fully to Christianity and, on the other, is needlessly cruel to a fellow human. Other of Deloney's female characters shun male suitors because the men are ugly or poor or ill-mannered, but Winifred shuns Sir Hugh not for any of these reasons, or even because she wants to devote her life to good works rather than to one man. Winifred spends her life in silent meditation because, as she says, "My love is fled to heaven" (p. 76; sig. B1). On the other hand, Winifred is very much like other of Deloney's women. Like John Winchcombe's first wife, she acts to regulate her suitor's excesses and like Thomas Cole's wife, she holds to principles of right action even in the face of death. She is part of Deloney's ordered cosmos.

Sir Hugh is somewhat more complex than Winifred. He does try to reason out Winifred's motivations and moods. Again, he is tempted to condemn all women as inconstant, and he leaves England to seek a land where there are no women. When in Italy he finds the women friendly to him and is suspicious of them, he recognizes the ambiguity in his thinking. He is angry at Winifred for being cold toward him, and now finds himself angry at the Italian women for their warmth. But Sir Hugh is not always so analytical. When Winifred is moved to honor him for his martyrdom, Sir Hugh answers, "I neuer loued truly vntill thou taughtest me to loue" (p. 85; sig. C2). What he means by "love" is not very clear, since all she has done for him is to help get him condemned to death. When he is forced by the tyrant to drink the blood of Winifred, Sir Hugh welcomes her "sweet blood . . . precious and pure" (p. 86; sig. C2v). The fact that her blood has been laced with deadly poison seems to be a detail that escapes him. Although Hugh "loves" Winifred enough to want to join her in death, he cannot refer to her blood as "precious and pure" without appearing foolish.

A more interesting love story is told when Deloney leaves the artificiality of romance and turns to the more realistic courting of shoemakers and their young maidens. When Simon Eyre's journeymen John, Haunce, and Nicholas vie for the love of Florence, they encounter complications just as Sir Hugh did. The dangers they face, however, are not from dragons and stiff-jointed elephants but from plots, stratagems, and misunderstandings they themselves create. Winifred spurns Sir Hugh because she wants to devote herself to some abstract spiritual idea; but Florence, who has no aversion to loving a mortal man, is wary of all three of her suitors because she knows too little about them to trust them. In the end Florence trusts the wisdom of Master Eyre and marries the man whose language and culture are closest to her own. She and Nicholas do not die for a high ideal after having pledged their chaste love with a chaste kiss. They are set up in business and presumably live realistically ever after.

Even the love story of Ursula and Crispine is more realistic than that of Winifred and Sir Hugh. Ursula and Crispine are of noble birth, and Ursula does have a romantic turn of mind. But Crispine's romanticism, if indeed he is ever afflicted with it, is tempered with the necessities of his duties in the shoemaker's shop. When asked by Ursula what kind of wife he wants, Crispine answers, "If I were to chuse a wife, then would I haue one faire, rich, and wise; first to delight mine eye, secondly, to supply my want, and thirdly, to gouern my house" (p. 96; sig. D4). Ursula admits that she "will die rather than liue without thee" (p. 96; sig. D4) and asks Crispine if he can "be contented to die for a Ladies loue" (p. 96; sig. D4). Crispine's answer sets him apart from the love-sick Sir Hugh; he answers, "No Madam (quoth he) if I could keep her loue and liue" (p. 96; sig. D4).

Probably Deloney's best-drawn characters—and his most famous— are Simon Eyre and his wife. To be sure, Deloney strains verisimilitude by having the Eyres become too famous too fast; the Lord Mayor invites Eyre to dinner and treats him as an old friend even before Eyre has received any money from the sale of the ship's treasure. But Deloney creates in the Eyre household a useful, happy family where the husband and wife have great affection and respect for each other and a sense of responsibility for the journeymen and apprentices who live and work with them.

Eyre is, like John Winchcombe and Thomas Cole, the master of his house and shop, with all of the rights and responsibilities the position involves. The two previous episodes in *The Gentle Craft, Part 1* have examples of pope-like tyrants whom the craftsmen must either fight against or deceive in order to survive, governors different from the enlightened kings in the first two novels. Henry VIII and Henry I, as Deloney presented them, are more chairmen of the commonwealth, governing with the advice and consent of the other classes, especially the middle class. No king appears in the Simon Eyre episode, probably because Eyre rises to the position of Lord Mayor and thus becomes the ruler figure for Deloney's purposes. Eyre displays the characteristics of both the enlightened monarch and the responsible tradesman. As Lord Mayor, he respects the worth of the workers, is aware of their needs, is on familiar terms with both workers and nobility, and in general cooperates with all segments of society for the common good. As tradesman, he listens to advice from his wife and journeymen so that he can operate a prosperous business. Deloney's model of the ideal family is best shown in the relationship between Eyre and his wife.

Eyre's wife knows her husband's weaknesses and does not hesitate to guide him in matters ranging from business to proper dress. Eyre, for his part, is tolerant of his wife's incessant chatter about such things as their reception at the Lord Mayor's house because he loves her without reservation and because he is wise enough to learn from her. Although he is greatly honored by the social elite of London, his devotion to his wife and to their simple lifestyle never changes. Certainly the most touching scene in all of Deloney's works is that in which Eyre presents his "little table" to the Alderman of London. Eyre's wife is ashamed to reveal something so insignificant to their honored guests, but Eyre's love for his wife is so great that it takes precedence over any honor he can receive in society. It is with great pride that he spreads a napkin over his wife's lap and serves his guests from the "little table" he will not give up "for a thousand pounds" (p. 123; sig. H2v). His "honored guests" are no better than he and his wife. In Deloney's democratic society there are different classes with different duties. But they are all part of the commonwealth and equal in respect to usefulness.

The great variety of language used in *The Gentle Craft, Part 1* indicates Deloney's versatility as a writer. The literary style of the day was euphuism, and Deloney's romantic characters are in style. The tales of Sir Hugh and of Crispine and Crispianus are full of courtly rhetoric and euphuistic elements. The typical courtly lover bewails his "troubled stars" in "the winter of my woes" because of "such corrupt cattell" as women are. This speech by Sir Hugh is typical of the balanced construction, alliteration, far-fetched comparisons, and other euphuistic elements Deloney borrows from Lyly to use in his tales of high romance:

I trust (my Deare) that now the Destinies haue yeelded a conuenient opportunity for me to finish my long begun sute, with the end of my former sorrowes. Long and tedious hath the winter of my woes beene, which with nipping care hath blasted the beauty of my youthfull delight, which is like neuer again to flourish, except the bright Sunshine of thy fauour doe renew the same: therefore (fair Loue) remember thy promise made vnto me, and put me no more off with vnpleasing delayes.

(p. 76; sig. A4v)

The speeches of Winifred are no less affected, and only slightly less are those of Crispine, Crispianus, and Ursula. But while Deloney's "euphuistic excursions" are neither extreme nor unpleasant even to a modern reader, his best work, indeed his uniqueness, is seen in his tales of the conflicts and resolutions involving the members of and pretenders to the middle class. Simon Eyre's language is clear, concise, and free of either the elaborate ornamentation of euphuism or the crudities and slang of the lower classes. Eyre's speeches reveal a clarity and dignity comparable to those of the Mayor and Aldermen of the city. When Eyre is offered the position of Sheriff, for example, he refuses politely, but succinctly and clearly:

My good Lord (quoth he) I humbly thank the City for their courtesie and kindnesse, and would to God my wealth were answerable to my good will, and my ability were able to bear it. But I find my selfe insufficient; I most humbly desire a yeers respite more, and pardon for this present.

(p. 123; sig. H2v)

Less elegant than the courtly speeches and less clear than Eyre's speeches is the language of the foreign journeymen who people Eyre's shop. Deloney had experimented with the vulgar western dialect of Mistress Winchcombe's father in *Jack of Newbury* and the broad northern dialect of Hodgekins in *Thomas of Reading*. But the dialect most useful in the creation of broad farce proved to be the reproduction of the broken English of foreign journeymen, as can be seen in the episodes involving Benedick in *Jack of Newbury*. Deloney returns to the foreigner's use of English in *The Gentle Craft, Part 1*. Crude, inexact, full of foreign words and corrupted English, the speeches of John the Frenchman provide many comic scenes in Deloney's tale. When Haunce, in his plan to gull the Frenchman, tells John that Florence has called him "shitten John," John angrily denounces Florence and enlarges the argument begun by Haunce by saying, "Mordue me shall be reuenged, be Got: shitten *Iohn*? call a shitten *Iohn*, hea? A de put in corroyn, a meshant, shitten *Iohn*, no better name but shitten *Iohn*?" (p. 120; sig. H1).

John resents being called "shitten John," but he does not really understand what Haunce is telling him. Later when John asks Florence why she no longer drinks with him she shouts at him, "Go get thee hence, prating fool (quoth she) I drink with thee? Thou shalt be piepeckt first" (p. 125; sig. H4). John is not quite sure what "pie-peckt" means, but he knows that Florence will have nothing to do with him. And although the language used by John, Haunce, Nicholas, and Florence is direct enough, it adds to their problems, and the result is that their excursions into love are little more successful than that of St. Winifred and St. Hugh. Deloney's aversion to foreigners, as exemplified by his complaint against non-guild refugees in 1595, surely contributed to his portraying them often as buffoons.

Deloney's imagery in the three episodes which make up *The Gentle Craft, Part 1* is, like the language, appropriate to the characters and action of each part. Learned allusions and elaborate comparisons abound, especially in the episode of St. Winifred and St. Hugh. When Sir Hugh visits Venice, for example, he is accosted by "a crue of Court-like Dames" who "like deceiuing Syrens" sing a song to him in such a provocative manner "as had been sufficient to allure chast-hearted *Xenocrates* vnto folly" (p. 78; sig. B1v). When he decides to return to Winifred, hoping she has changed her mind, Sir Hugh can call up many analogies to support the possibility that Winifred might now be amenable to love:

The wildest Bull (quoth he) is tamed being tied to a Fig-tree, and the coyest Dame (in time) may yield like the stone Charachaedonis, which sparkles like fire, and yet melts at the touch of soft wax. Though Roses haue prickles, yet they are gathered; and though women seem froward, yet they will show themselues kind and friendly.

(p. 82; sig. B4)

The imagery in the episode of Crispine and Crispianus occurs primarily in the conversations between Crispine and Ursula; and although Crispine's thoughts and actions are less romantic than Sir Hugh's, the imagery he uses is often as elaborate as that in the story of Winifred and Sir Hugh. When Crispine explains to Ursula that he, like any normal man, is capable of love, he goes to great lengths to explain that love is natural:

. . . the Doue and the Peacock loue intirely, so doth the Turtle and the Popinjay; the like affection the fish Musculus beareth vnto the huge Whale, insomuch that he leadeth him from all danger of stony rocks; and as among birds and fishes, so amongst plants and trees the like concord is to be found; for if the male of palme trees be planted from the female, neither of both prosper: and being set one neer another, they flourish accordingly, imbracing with joy the branches one of the other.

(p. 95; sig. D3v)

The imagery, like the characters and language, in the story of Simon Eyre is not as elaborate as that in the two earlier episodes. Earthy language, rather than classical allusions, comes more naturally from the mouths of the members of the Eyre household. The images used by the craftsmen come from nature rather than from books. When John is angry at Florence, he looks at her "fierce as a Panther" (p. 121; sig. H1). Simon Eyre, telling his wife that he has a responsibility to share some of his wealth in service to the community, explains that he cannot be "like the Ebontree, that neither beares leafes nor fruit" (p. 132; sig. I3v). But never does Deloney fall into the trap of putting elaborate courtly conceits into the mouths of his working-class characters.

Courtly conceits and noble characters make up most of the first two episodes of *The Gentle Craft, Part 1*. Perhaps Deloney read the mood of the times accurately, for, of all his works, *The Gentle Craft, Part 1* has been the most popular from the time it was first published until well into the eighteenth century.[74] But the characters and language used in these episodes are little suited to the workaday world which Deloney knew best. The romantic episodes are weak imitations of a style used better by John Lyly, Philip Sidney, and other writers whose experience with lords and ladies was gained firsthand.

The strength of *The Gentle Craft, Part 1* lies in the scenes involving his middle-class characters, who face the thousand natural shocks that flesh is heir to. The story of Simon Eyre, for example, a story of a craftsman of good humor who elevates himself, his family, and his workers by his own hard labor, responsibility, and daring to a position of honor and comfort, is immediate, delightful, and instructive. Eyre's rise may exceed the successes achieved by John Winchcombe and Thomas Cole, though not by much. Both of the earlier two heroes became powerful and respected men in England. The theory that middle-class merchants could rise to positions of economic and political power—even that they could be heroes in a piece of serious literature—may be revolutionary. But in Deloney's fiction the revolution is not only bloodless, but clearly beneficial to the operation of a secure, progressive commonwealth. Eyre is given nothing; he earns his positions, his wealth, and his happiness; and he contributes as much to society as he gets from it.

Simon Eyre was a very popular character with Deloney's audiences well into the eighteenth century. Thomas Dekker turned to the episode of Simon Eyre for his famous play, *The Shoemakers' Holiday*, but Dekker's Eyre is significantly different from Deloney's character, and

Dekker's view of society was perhaps also different. According to Arthur F. Kinney, Dekker's play places "traditional order and obedience alongside social and economic mobility," not to show that they can work together but to advance "folly in order to exorcise it, permitting a Lord of Misrule the better to avow tradition."[75] Dekker's Eyre is a mock ruler, a "Lord of Misrule," who serves only to cleanse and reestablish the old tradition. Deloney's Eyre, however, is no mock hero, no Lord of Misrule. Deloney's social model is neither the old hierarchy nor a new mutable order. Neither is the one juxtaposed against the other. In Deloney's novels the two are merged. The permanence of a hierarchy in society is as necessary in Deloney's model as order in the macrocosm, astronomical or divine. There are in Deloney, as I have noted, separate classes in society, but insofar as they all support the commonwealth, they are equal. Deloney's Simon Eyre is the hero of the middle class and the new hero of novels. Moll Flanders, Tom Jones, and countless later characters follow in the line, not of St. Winifred and St. Hugh, but of Simon Eyre.

V The Gentle Craft, Part 2

A *The Sources*

Corresponding to the first part of *The Gentle Craft*, the second part consists of three distinct episodes unified only by the fact that they are about shoemakers. The first four chapters contain the story of Richard Casteler, a handsome shoemaker in Westminster, who is pursued by most of the single women of the town, but especially by Long Meg. The ensuing five chapters tell of the famous London shoemaker, Lusty Peachey, and his men. Two short final chapters are devoted to the story of another shoemaker, the Green King of St. Martin's. Deloney again takes the broad outline of his stories from the chronicles, jest books, plays, and poems of his time, but, as in his earlier works, he fleshes out the stories with local tradition, legends, and his own experiences with the working class.

The "History of Richard Casteler" comes from brief comments in Holinshed[76] and Grafton.[77] Both identify an industrious shoemaker from Westminster called "the Cocke of Westminster" because he regularly began his work at 4 A.M. An industrious and prosperous businessman who had no children, the historical Casteler and his wife gave valuable land to Christ's Hospital in order to benefit the poor and indigent. Holinshed describes him only briefly as a good man "whose example God grant manie to follow."[78] In his novel Deloney gives this historical shoemaker a voice, personality, and life.

Two other characters in this episode come from a variety of stories, poems, and legends about a certain Margaret, an Amazon of Westminster known as Long Meg, who according to many sources was a well-known prostitute.[79] Deloney ties the popular story of Long Meg to Richard Casteler by having her fall in love with him and then invents another woman, Gillian, to compete with Long Meg for Casteler's love. The shoemaker's companion, Round Robin, is probably drawn from a Dr. Skelton, who is mentioned in one of the popular tales of Long Meg.[80]

The episode concerning Lusty Peachey is composed from many brief episodes, each with its own plots and characters. No fewer than ten significant characters appear in the episode, but Peachey is its unifying character. The stories, as well as the characters themselves, come from a variety of sources: history, literature, and legend.[81] The names of John Peachey, Harry Neville, Richard Abridges, and Sir John Rainsford are mentioned in Holinshed and several other histories which were available to Deloney. The sea captains Stutely and Strangwidge are discussed in several chronicles and fictionalized in plays and ballads of the late sixteenth century. Dr. Burket and Alderman Jarvis are also characters drawn from such works as the *Life and Pranks of Long Meg of Westminster* (1582) and *Kind-Heartes Dream* (1592). Tom Drum is undoubtedly a traditional character in English legend, for "Tom Drum's entertainment" was a popular term for the reception given an unwelcome guest in a tavern or at a party.[82] Deloney simply takes this catalogue of characters and stories, shuffles them together, ties them to Lusty Peachey, and produces a complex episode for his novel about shoemakers. The fact that none of the characters or plots is remotely connected to shoemakers in the sources did not hinder Deloney. He merely makes the famous Sir John Peachey a master shoemaker and has the other characters wander in and out of his shop as employees or customers.

The character of the Green King of St. Martin's in the third episode of *The Gentle Craft, Part 2* has no obvious historical or literary source, but the story of the wastrel merchant laid low in fortune and raised back to success is a favorite motif of Deloney. It occurs in the episodes of Randoll Pert in *Jack of Newbury* and of Tom Dove in *Thomas of Reading*. Another character in the last episode, however, was probably well known to Deloney through tradition and contemporary reference. Anthony Now-now is described by Henry Chettle as a ballad-singer, whose "treble violl in his hands" denoted his profession.[83]

What Deloney borrows from his sources are primarily the names of characters who would be well known to his audience. As Hyder Rollins has demonstrated, Deloney obviously owed his euphuistic references to natural history to Stephen Batman, Thomas Fortescue, and Thomas Johnson.[84] But almost never does Deloney borrow the story or language verbatim. Such borrowings would have been difficult in some cases: Holinshed, Grafton, and Stow, for example, report the main events in the lives of men of historical significance, but rarely do these chroniclers analyze the characters of these men, and even more rarely do they record dialogue. The same is true of characters and events found in ballads and jest books. A close comparison of Deloney's work to his sources, such as those by Mann and Rollins, reveals that any attempt to decide how Deloney modified his sources, changed their tone, or made them in some way better or worse is fruitless. His stories come primarily from legend, tradition, and the streets of London; he merely borrows names and places from popular literature to weave into his tales. Mann is correct in saying that "Deloney's use of printed sources must not be over-emphasized."[85]

B   The Plot

In the first episode Long Meg and Gillian, two maidens in Westminster, attempt to woo Richard Casteler, a handsome young shoemaker. Each woman visits Richard, brings food for him, sends him wine, and generally tries to persuade the young man that she is the better one for him. At the same time, each woman does her best to thwart the suit of the other. Richard has no romantic interest in either Meg or Gillian, but Round Robin, his co-worker, urges Richard to allow him to deceive the women for sport and profit. On the pretense of arguing the case of each one, Robin eats their food, drinks their wine, and makes each think that Richard is in love with her.

In the meantime, Richard falls in love with a Dutch maiden in London and persuades her to marry him. Meg and Gillian are so melancholy at their loss that Robin gives each a willow garland, a symbol of forsaken love. Gillian resolves to die and goes to bed. Meg, resolving to live, persuades Gillian to go with her to Richard's wedding wearing their garlands. Richard's bride apologizes to the two maidens and blames her husband for his unkindness. Long Meg leaves Westminster to follow the King's army as a prostitute, and Gillian marries well. Richard becomes a master shoemaker and, dying childless, leaves his fortune to the poor.

In the second episode Lusty Peachey, a rich shoemaker in London, keeps in his shop forty workers to whom he has given rich clothes and swords. When Stutely and Strangwidge, two sea captains, see Peachey and his men calling upon the Duke of Suffolk, they are enraged to see commoners dress and act like noblemen. The sea captains visit Peachey's shop to insult the workers, but they are soundly beaten for their insults. Peachey's men defeat Stutely and Strangwidge regularly in numerous duels, causing the noblemen to wish they had never insulted the valiant shoemakers. Peachey finally ends the dispute at the request of the Duke of Suffolk.

Because Peachey's reputation is great throughout England, many shoemakers seek to work for him; among them is Tom Drum of Petworth, a boasting, cozening journeyman. On his way to London, Tom meets Harry Neville, a penniless young nobleman who had quarreled with his father and left home. Tom promises to teach Harry the trade of shoemaking if Harry will make him a gentleman. They agree to be friends and set off toward Peachey's shop in London.

The courageous and popular Sir John Rainsford happens upon a young widow and her five children begging a priest to bury her husband and pray for his soul. Because she has no money, the priest refuses. Enraged, Sir John has his men toss the villainous priest into a grave and cover him. Calling another priest, Sir John sees that the husband receives a Christian burial. But because the King issues a warrant to arrest him for murder, Sir John is forced to disguise himself as one of Peachey's shoemakers. Sir John is pardoned by the King when he performs valiantly in a battle against the French.

Harry Neville falls in love with a beautiful widow, Mistress Farmer, but finds that he is in competition with Dr. Burket and Alderman Jarvis. As the suitors plan and scheme against each other, the widow falls in love with a worthy apprentice who works for her. Harry is so grieved that he leaves Peachey's service and becomes an apprentice in several other trades. When his father dies, leaving his fortune to his only son, Harry pays all his old debts to his respected former comrades.

In the third episode Deloney tells the brief story of "The Green King," a shoemaker in St. Martin's. He spends on his friends more than he earns and thus is in debt. When he seeks help from his friends, they abandon him. In order to regain his fortune he decides to travel to Holland, leaving his business in the hands of his wife. On his way the Green King meets Anthony, the fiddler, who offers to buy his friend a pint of wine and to play him some music. The song he composes for the shoemaker has for its refrain, "O Anthony, now, now, now." The song becomes so popular that the musician becomes known as "Anthony Now-now."

While he is gone, the shoemaker's wife tends so carefully to business that she is able to recover their lost fortune. When the Green King returns home, he finds that his neighbors, who had refused to help him while he was in need, now salute and flatter him. The shoemaker warns his dishonest neighbors to stay clear of his long sword. So devoted is he to his wife, however, that when she complains that he never takes her walking with him, the Green King promises to allow her to walk with him to St. James Fair. He also asks several other shoemakers to accompany him, making them post a £20 bond that they will walk with him the entire distance. With Anthony Now-now, the group sets off to the fair, but the Green King announces that he intends to walk to the fair in Bristol, not the one in Westminster as they had expected. He thus gives his wife and his neighbors more than enough walking.

Tom Drum returns from the Scottish wars to work for the Green King. Tom claims credit for the actions of other men in battle. His lies become so gross that no one can believe him. The Green King lives a long and prosperous life, dying after he has done much to aid the poor.

C   *Analysis*

Deloney's purpose in *The Gentle Craft, Part 2* is primarily to glorify the members of England's gentle craft, the shoemakers. Nowhere in this work does Deloney digress to insert improbable romantic stories of lords and ladies beset with monsters or tyrants. Harry Neville and Sir John Rainsford are the only noblemen playing major roles, and even they are totally involved in bourgeois life. Although the craft of shoemaking is only incidental to many of the tales, the life described is consistently middle-class. The episodes are primarily anecdotal, more so than in any of Deloney's previous works, but his theme is the same. His craftsmen heroes, all "gentlemen by condition," are valuable members of a complex society which exists for the common good.

The opening episode of Richard Casteler, like that of Simon Eyre in Part 1, is well organized and unified. Margaret, Gillian, and Round

Robin are all tied to Casteler, the successful young shoemaker, who lives a prosperous life and does much to aid the poor. The second episode, about the famous, if imaginary shoemaker, Lusty Peachey, is much more episodic. Using the same structure as in *Thomas of Reading*, Deloney relates the stories of a variety of characters only incidentally connected to Peachey. His method of transition from one episode to another is, however, smoother than any found in *Thomas of Reading*. After establishing Peachey as the central character by having him achieve fame in his defeat of Stutely and Strangwidge, for example, Deloney deftly works his way into the episode with Tom Drum. So famous had the shoemaker˙ Lusty Peachey become that

> . . . it made many of that occupation desirous to come and dwell with him, for beside that he was a good tall man of his hands, he was also an excellent good workman, and therewithall a bountifull house keeper. Among many other that was desirous of his service there was one called *Tom Drum*, that had a great minde to be his man, a very odde fellow, and one that was sore infected with the sin of cogging [deceiving].
>
> (p. 175; sig. F3v)

The final episode, much shorter than the other two, is also much less complex. The story of the Green King is made up of two parts: the reverse-success formula Deloney had already used in the stories of Randoll Pert in *Jack of Newbury* and Tom Dove in *Thomas of Reading* and a jest that the shoemaker plays on his wife and some friends.

Richard Casteler, Deloney's craftsman-hero in the first episode, has most of the same qualities as John Winchcombe, Thomas Cole, and Simon Eyre. He is, according to Long Meg, "a gentle young man, curteous and kind, diligent about his business, and wary in his dealings, which argues good husbandry" (p. 145; sig. B1v), and is thus a valuable member of the commonwealth. But his support for the King is limited to his sending his workers to sing for the royal company. He does not advise the King or send soldiers to the wars as his predecessors did. His major contributions to the commonwealth occur not during his life, but at his death:

> . . . at his death he did diuers good and godly deeds: among many other things he gaue to the City of *Westminster* a worthy gift to the cherishing of the poore inhabitants for euer. He also gaue toward the reliefe of the poore fatherlesse children of *Christs Hospitall in London*, to the value of forty pound land by the yeere; and in the whole course of his life he was a very

bountifull man to all the decayed housekeepers of that place, leauing behind
him a worthy example for other men to follow.

(p. 170; sig. E4v)

Deloney's purpose in the Richard Casteler episode seems to be more
to present "matters of merriment" (p. 140; sig. A2v), as he says in his
preface, than to create a model hero. Long Meg and Gillian are at least
as important in Deloney's story as the hero. Where Deloney is most
consistent with his earlier works is in settings. The characters may be
drawn from history or from jest books, but their conflicts are set against
a background of pragmatic middle-class life. Meg and Gillian are
women in love, but they do not wander in a pastoral glade hanging
love sonnets on trees. As much as Gillian wants a rendezvous with Richard Casteler, she is painfully aware that she has clothes to wash. She
does neglect her chores to chase Casteler, but such irresponsibility is
what causes the industrious shoemaker to shun her as a wife. Unlike
characters in medieval romances, she and Long Meg do not die of broken hearts when they are thwarted in love. Gillian tries to play the role
of the wounded lover, but Long Meg soon talks her out of such silliness.
She does not enter a convent to spend the rest of her life in meditation,
as Margaret does in *Thomas of Reading;* nor does she bid her love
farewell while her blood drains from her open veins, as does Winifred
in *The Gentle Craft, Part 1.* Gillian recovers and, true to the practical
middle class, we are told,

Gillian in the end was well married, and became a very good house-keeper,
living in honest name and fame till her dying day.

(p. 166; sig. E2)

Although all the characters are either shoemakers or in some way
associated with shoemakers, they are nevertheless individualized. Each
has his own personality with his own humor, his own identity, just as
the real people in the workshops must have had. Long Meg and Gillian,
for example, are both servants of comparable talents, both earn a comfortable living, and both pursue Richard Casteler. But they are very
different characters. Gillian is less bold, more self-protective. She hes-
itates to slight her duties to her employer in order to pursue Richard,
and she decides to do so only when there seems to be no other possibility. When she is rejected, she hides in her bed hoping she will die.
Long Meg, on the other hand, is willing to be as bold as she has to be.

Not only is she not ashamed to show both her foot and her leg to Richard, but she also takes no offense at Robin's bawdy suggestion that she has provided sexual entertainment for more men than she can count. When her master sits on the hot posset, Meg does not hesitate to lift his night shirt and spread salad oil on his buttocks. When she is spurned by Richard, having tried the socially acceptable ways of getting a man, she boldly sets out to lose her virginity as rapidly as possible. Angry that she has wasted so much time being "so dainty of my maidenhead," she promises to be even bolder:

> ... what a deale of time haue I lost and spent to no purpose since I came to *London?* and how many kinde offers haue I forsaken and disdainfully refused of many braue Gentlemen, that would haue bin glad of my good will? I thinke I was accurst to come into his company: Well, I say little, but henceforward hang me if I refuse reason, when I am reasonably intreated.
>
> (p. 166; sig. E2)

One scene in particular serves to show the boldness of Long Meg and the timidity of Gillian. Gillian admits that although her maidenhead is "somewhat burdensom to beare" (p. 142; sig. A4), she has refused many offers of marriage. Long Meg then captivates Gillian with a vivid description of the joys of marriage. A husband will speak sweetly to his wife, serve her a cup of good wine, and feed her the best parts of a chicken. If the wife wants anything, the husband will see that she has it. When the meal is finished, he will set her on his knee, amorously chuck her under the chin, and kiss her. As soon as he hears the clock strike eight, he will call her to bed. These are the sweetest words in a woman's ear, declares Long Meg. And when they are between a pair of sheets, says Meg provocatively, "O Gillian, then, then." Gillian, enraptured, whispers timidly, "Why what of that?" Long Meg answers coquettishly, "Nay nothing . . . but they sleep soundly all night" (p. 143; sig. A4v).

Richard refuses to marry either Meg or Gillian because neither possesses the qualities of a good wife. While Richard is working long hours to establish himself in his business, the two women are neglecting their duties to chase him, spending money foolishly, and deceiving their masters and each other. He turns instead to a young Dutch maiden "who . . . was of proper personage, and comely countenance, and could doe diuers pretty feates to get her owne liuing" (p. 155; sig. C3). In the tradition of John Winchcombe and the shoemaker-prince Crispine, the industrious Richard chooses his wife pragmatically. Richard gets involved with Meg and Gillian not because he is interested; his man Robin persuades him to let him gull the women.

Robin's most immediately noticeable trait is his habit of speaking almost exclusively in rhyme, but there is more to the man's character than a habit of speech. He takes great delight in playing tricks upon the forward "girles of Westminster" who have thought so little of him as to try to bribe him in plots against his master, Richard Casteler, for Robin is steadfastly devoted to his employer. When Richard chides Robin for playing tricks on Gillian and Long Meg, Robin tries to explain that he is merely trying to aid his friend:

> Thus you doe neuer esteeme of a man,
> Let him doe for you the best that he can.
> (p. 158; sig. D1v)

Richard, perceiving that his friend is hurt and angry, goes to great lengths to pacify him. Robin returns Richard's friendship with consistent loyalty. When the King rewards Robin for his rhyming and singing, Robin's first thought is to use his share of the money to buy dinner for his master.

The story of Peachey is the most complex of the episodes in *The Gentle Craft, Part 2*. The central character is a worthy craftsman— the industrious, responsible, orderly commonwealth man Deloney creates for his model societies. He provides economic stability in the land by keeping a large work force of well-paid craftsmen. He discharges his professional obligations by seeing that members of the cordwainer's guild, such as Tom Drum, are properly employed. He goes beyond his own profession in this matter by taking into his service those who, while not shoemakers, are in need. Both Harry Neville and Sir John Rainsford are welcomed into Peachey's house. And finally, Peachey discharges his political obligations by providing thirty of his own men, with himself as their captain, for the King in his war with France.

In this episode Deloney creates characters who are examples of both the commonwealth man and his opposite. Peachey, as I have noted, is Deloney's ideal merchant. Industrious and responsible, he earns the good life he lives. When the haughty sea captains, Stutely and Strangwidge, seek to harass Peachey, the shoemaker explains that because he is as good as any man, he does not stand in awe of their nobility:

Sir (quoth *Peachie*) you wrong me too much, and get you quickly from my doore, or, by this sunne that shines, ile set you packing, & therefore neuer think to outface me with great looks, for I tell thee *Stutely* and *Strangwidge* both, did you look as big as the Deuill I feare you not. And you forgot your manners too much to giue me such base tearms, for I would you well knew, I keepe forty good fellows in my house, that in respect of their manhood may seeme to your equals.

(p. 173; sig. F2)

When the sea captains are beaten soundly and consistently in the art of fencing, not only by Peachey, but also by various of Peachey's men, the proud gentlemen learn that the shoemakers are worthy men and decide to seek their friendship. In order to cease the fight which they had begun, Stutely and Strangwidge are forced to ask Peachey's friend, the Duke of Suffolk, to intervene. The idea of the commonwealth is restored when the sea captains treat the shoemakers with the respect due deserving members of society.

The story of Harry Neville also reinforces Deloney's idea of the importance of earned rewards in society. Harry is a prodigal son, having displeased his parents and run away from home. Since he has no marketable skills, he is destitute when Tom Drum happens upon him. Peachey takes him in, but Harry is not an apt worker at anything he tries, be it shoemaking, goldsmithing, barbering, cooking, comfitmaking, or blacksmithing. He is provided for by the various merchants because, as responsible members of the commonwealth, they have an obligation to see that everyone is cared for. Unemployment in late sixteenth-century England was a chronic problem, but in Deloney's model system, even a displaced and inept gentleman can find employment. Tom Drum explains the system to Harry:

Tush (quoth Tom) shoomakers will not see one another lacke, for it is our vse if wee know of a good fellow that comes to towne, wanting either meate or money, and that he make himselfe knowne, he shall neede to take no further care, for he shall be sure that the iourneymen of that place will not onely giue him kinde welcome, but also prouide him all things necessary of free cost: And if he be disposed to worke among them, he shall haue a Master prouided by their meanes, without any sute made by himselfe at all.

(p. 178; sig. G1)

And in Deloney's works the system operates precisely as Tom says. Harry is so impressed by the reasonableness of the system that when he inherits his father's fortune, he repays all his former masters for the wrongs he had done them, "And euer after, this Gentleman kept men of all these occupations in his own house" (p. 203; sig. K4v).

Harry's failure to win the hand of the rich widow, Mistress Farmer, is caused by his (and Tom Drum's) bumbling lack of responsibility. A physician and an alderman who court the widow also fail, less because of their bad qualities than because of the good qualities of the servant William, her choice for husband. As the widow in *Jack of Newbury* chooses John Winchcombe as a husband because of his qualities as a loyal, industrious, and responsible craftsman, and as John later chooses the servant girl for his mate because she has those same qualities, Mistress Farmer shuns her higher-class suitors in favor of the competent, loyal William. Calling him from the kitchen where she had banished him as a means of testing him, she announces to the horror of her dinner guests that she will marry the scullion, "his face all begrimed, and his cloathes all greasie":

> Good Lord my masters, how much do your sights deceiue you? in my sight he looks the loueliest of them all, hauing a pleasant countenance, and a good grace, and so pleasing is he in euery part to my sight, that surely if hee will accept of mee for his wife, I will not refuse him for my husband.
>
> (p. 201; sig. K3)

Because of their devotion to the orderly commonwealth, therefore, Peachey, Sir John, Mistress Farmer, William, and even Harry Neville all lead secure and happy lives.

The Green King, hero of the last episode, fits Deloney's model also, in the same way that Randoll Pert did in *Jack of Newbury*. A competent craftsman and a successful businessman, the Green King revels with his neighbors and begins to neglect his business. The story of the businessman who is brought low by being too generous and who is later restored to his former fortune is a favorite theme of Deloney's. But although the Green King is in some ways like other of Deloney's characters, in other ways he is unique. His green satin clothes illustrate his flair for the unusual. His habit of carrying a two-handed sword with him wherever he goes demonstrates pride and independence. When his friends disappear along with his fortune, the Green King does not sink into despair as others might have done. He condemns his false friends and shuns them when his fortune returns. Only his wife and the minstrel Anthony Now-now are decent enough to remain loyal to

the shoemaker through his financial troubles, and only his wife and
Anthony Now-now receive the benefits of the Green King's new
fortune.

The place of the wife in middle-class life is emphasized once again
in the episode of the Green King. In each of his novels, as well as in
several of his ballads, Deloney presents the wife as a partner in the
business as well as in the family. John Winchcombe's success was due
in large measure to the influence of his two wives, and Thomas Cole's
wife was able to continue her husband's contributions to society after
his death because she possessed the same qualities that made her husband a valuable member of the commonwealth. Simon Eyre's wife
directed him to a fortune and advised him in both personal and business matters. Deloney reveals, perhaps autobiographically, in "Salomon's good housewife" his admiration of a good wife, as I have
discussed. The Green King's wife is in the tradition of Deloney's good
housewives, for more important than his wealth or his reputation
among his neighbors was "that God blest him with the gift of a good
wife, who was a very comely young woman, and therewithall very
carefull for his commoditie" (p. 203; sig. K4v).

The language the characters speak in *The Gentle Craft, Part 2* is
the clear idiomatic language of Renaissance England. The fact that the
middle-class Englishman of Deloney's time studied to "conform to the
manner of speech practiced by those who had arrived socially"[86] is
clearly illustrated in the speeches of the various craftsmen and their
servants. When Gillian of the George wants to explain to Long Meg
why she has not yet married, she can express her ideas clearly:

You did euen now demand a question of me, and very desirous you were to
know why I did not marry when I was so well offered: Trust me *Margaret*,
I take you to be my friend which makes me the more willing to vnfold my
fancy, being as well persuaded of your secresie as I am of your amity, and
there-vpon I am the more willing to make you copartner of my counsailes.
Fire in straw will not be hidden, and the flames of affection will burst forth
at length, though it be long kept vnder. And truth it is that I haue forsaken
good matches, for I might haue had Master *Cornelius* of the Guard if I
would, who as you know is wealthy, and therwithall of very good conuersa-
tion, yet there was one thing make me refuse his kind offer.

What was that (quoth *Margaret*) I pray thee tell? (Quoth she) he loued not
me so well but I loued another tenne times better, and therefore it is not good
for handes to ioyne, where heartes agree not.

(pp. 143–144; sig. A4v)

Although Gillian borrows a common proverb to make her point,[87] there is here none of the overly ornamented finery of euphuism found to some extent in all of Deloney's earlier novels. He even abandons the harshness of vulgar bombast and the strangeness of unfamiliar dialects, experiments in dialogue which were relatively successful in the earlier works. In his last novel Deloney seems determined to present only those characters who have "arived socially," at least insofar as language is concerned.

Round Robin's trick of speaking in rhyme, however, adds little that is either pleasant or instructive to Deloney's work. Using a predominantly iambic pattern in couplets, Robin necessarily becomes known as one who "would scant speake anything but in rime" (p. 147; sig. B3). This trait, like the Green King's green habit or Anthony Now-now's "Anthony now now," is only an idiosyncrasy which separates an otherwise ordinary craftsman from his fellows and gives the reader something to recognize and remember. Were it not for Robin's habit of speech, in time the reader might forget him. But although the device is merely a superficial technique of characterization, Deloney nevertheless blends both Robin and his rhyme neatly into the tale. Instead of having Robin deliver long speeches in couplets, Deloney uses the rhyme in dialogue, often even using stichomythia to add variety to conversations. Complaining at one point because he has not been offered any of the wine Long Meg and Richard Casteler are drinking, he says,

> *Much good doe it you masters, and well may you fare,*
> *Beshroe both your hearts and if you do spare:*
> *The wine should be nought as I judge by the smell,*
> *And by the colour too I know it full well.*
> Nay faith (quoth *Meg*) thats but a jest,
> *Ile sweare (quoth Robin) tis none of the best.*
> Tast it (quoth *Meg*) then tell me thy mind:
> *Yea marry (quoth Robin) now you are kind.*
> With that *Margaret* filling a cup brim full, gaue
> it into his hand saying: Now tast it *Robin* and take there the cup.
> *Nay hang me (quoth Robin) if I drinke it not vp.*
> By my Maiden-head (quoth *Margaret*) I see that thou art a good
> fellow: and to haue thee drinke it vp, is the thing that I craue.
> *Then sweare (quoth Robin) by the thing you haue,*
> *For this to sweare I dare be bold:*
> *You were a maid at three yeares old.*

> *From three to foure, fiue, sixe, and seauen,*
> *But when you grew to be eleuen,*
> *Then you began to breed desire;*
> *By twelve your fancy was on fire:*
> *At thirteene yeares desire grew quicke,*
> *And then your maiden-head fell sicke.*
> *But when you came vnto fourteene,*
> *All secret kisses was not seene:*
> *By that time fifteene yeares was past,*
> *I guesse your maiden-head was lost.*
> *And I pray God forgiue me this,*
> *If thinking so I thinke amisse.*

(pp. 147–148; sig. B3)

Robin is thus distinguished from Richard and Margaret, and indeed from the dozens of other apprentice shoemakers, clothiers, drapers, and various other craftsmen created by Deloney. Robin's trick of language, however affected, never overpowers the tale, as the longer ballads sometimes intrude on and displace the narrative in *Jack of Newbury*, or as the poems seem to take over from the prose story in Gascoigne's *Master F. J.* And because Robin keeps his ideas close to epigrammatic, the rhymed couplets are able to carry his meaning without difficulty. It is perhaps too much to believe that the King would want to reward Round Robin for being especially witty, but Robin is an interesting character, and his language helps to make him that.

Language is used, however, as one illustration of the worth of William, servant-suitor to Mistress Farmer. Not only is William loyal and humble, but his manner of speech shows that he is courteous, educated, and thoughtful. When he first reveals his love to his mistress, he speaks as decorously as any honest courtier:

Dear Mistris, needs must I proue both blinde in sight, and dull in conceipt, while your faire eyes that giues light to the Sunne obscure themselues, and dark the glory of their shine, when I seek to receiue comfort thereby; and the want of your good will makes my wits so weak, that like a barren tree it yields no fruit at all.

(p. 198; sig. K1v)

The imagery in *The Gentle Craft, Part 2* is more like that of *Jack of Newbury* than that of *Thomas of Reading*. That is, the characters in this novel appropriately draw their images not from the gods of classical antiquity or from the figures of pastoral romance, but from their own experience. Long Meg, for example, mentions maidenhead regularly in conversation as a symbol of her honesty, because as one might assume she consistently has her loss of it on her mind. Like Gillian, Meg finds her maidenhead a useless burden. When she describes Richard Casteler's relationship with Gillian, Meg insists that "he keeps all his gownes for Gillian of the George" (p. 148; sig. B3v), suggesting that he stains his clothes by rolling with her on the grass.[88] More veiled is her invitation to Richard to come into her "office," suggesting at least to Robin that she is inviting him to engage in sex with her:

> But tell vs first (quoth Robin) hath your office neuer a fire?
> Yfaith no (quoth she) you see the kitchen is large and the chimney wide:
> But how many rookes (quoth Robin) hath the goodness of your kitchen tride?
> I know not (said Meg) how many or how few:
> Trust me (quoth Robin) I thinke even so.
>
> (p. 153; sig. C2)

Gillian's images of love are less bold than Meg's turning as she does to familiar proverbs, as opposed to Meg's references to sex. "Loue," she says, "is like an vnruly streame that will ouer-flow the banks if the course be stopt" (p. 151; sig. C1).[89] Richard Casteler shuns both women saying that "a man must not be won with faire words as a fish with a baite" (p. 152; sig. C1v) and "the loue of a shroe is like the shadow of a cloude that consumeth as soone as it is seene" (p. 152; sig. C2). Their loves are, he says, "Like braided wares" (P. 158; sig. D1). The unhappy Meg and Gillian thus shunned, seek "Harts-ease" and find "nothing but sorrel," a bitter plant (p. 160; sig. D2v).[90]

When Harry Neville falls in love with Mistress Farmer, Deloney waxes more courtly, since Neville is a nobleman. Finding "his heart fired with the bright beams of this blazing Comet," Neville is wounded by Cupid. But common men in Deloney's novels describe their predicament with more common images. When William tells his friend Francis of his fear that if Doctor Burket and Alderman Jarvis cannot win the widow's love then surely he has no chance, Francis uses food imagery to show William's misunderstanding of human nature:

What a bad reason is this (quoth Francis) some cannot abide to eate of a Pig: some to taste of an Eele, othersome are sicke if they see but a Crab, and diuers cannot away with cheese; yet none of them all but doe liue by their victuals; euery man hath his fancy, & euery woman will follow her own mind, and therefore, though she find not an Alderman or a Doctor for her diet yet she may think William her man a fit morsell for her own tooth.

(p. 193; sig. I2v)

In this last novel Deloney makes no attempt to change the methods of characterization, imagery, or plot development that he found acceptable in his earlier efforts. The most important differences between this last novel and his earlier ones are the obvious parallels between *The Gentle Craft, Part 2* and Shakespeare's *1 Henry IV*.

Deloney's emphasis upon the individual scene in his prose works and his reliance upon dialogue as a means of advancing the narrative show the influence of drama upon him. But rarely does he transfer words and form from a play to be used in his prose, as he does in *The Gentle Craft, Part 2*. Long Meg's speech on grief is in both form and content the same as Falstaff's soliloquy on honor in *1 Henry IV*. Since honor can harm him but in no way help him, Falstaff very realistically refuses to have anything to do with it:

Can honor set to a leg? No. Or an arm? No. Or take away the grief of a wound? No. Honor hath no skill in surgery, then? No. What is honor? A word. What is in that word honor? What is that honor? Air. A trim reckoning! Who hath it? He that died o'Wednesday. Doth he feel it? No. Doth he hear it? No. 'Tis insensible, then? Yea, to the dead. But will it not live with the living? No. Why? Detraction will not suffer it. Therefore I'll none of it. Honor is a mere scutcheon. And so ends my catechism.

(V. i. 132–143)

Meg, no less realistic than Falstaff, uses the same catechism–like form in deciding that, since grief can harm but not help her, she will not grieve:

... wherefore is griefe good? can it recall folly? no; can it helpe a matter remedilesse? no: can it restore losses, or draw vs out of danger? no: can it bring long life? no: for it doth rather hasten our death, what then can it do: can it call our friends out of their graues? no: can it restore virginity if we chance to lose our maiden head? no: Then wherefore should I grieue? except I want to kill myselfe: Nay seeing it is so, hang sorrow, I will neuer care for them that care not for mee.

(p. 162; sig. D3v)

A character even more like Falstaff than Meg can also be found in
The Gentle Craft, Part 2. But if Long Meg profits from Falstaff's wisdom, Tom Drum follows the fat knight down trouble's road. In the
manner of Falstaff, Tom depends upon boasts, lies, jokes, and half-
truths to acquire a reputation as a man worthy of respect. He seeks the
company of noblemen and other men of good reputation so that he
may borrow their names. In one case, he actually borrows a gentleman's clothing when he gets Harry Neville to exchange clothes with
him.

Perhaps by creating a Falstaffian character of his own, facing him
with the same kinds of conflicts, and showing his readers that such a
delightful rogue can live a full and happy life among craftsman, Deloney is showing the benefits of the life of an artisan as contrasted to the
life of a politician. Falstaff, because he cannot measure up to Hal's
standard of nobility, is banished until he can conform to an acceptable,
and certainly more boring, standard of conduct. There are at least two
analogues to the out-of-favor nobleman in *The Gentle Craft, Part 2.*
First, Harry Neville is a nobleman who has "displeased his parents"
and is therefore "vtterly vndone" (p. 177; sig. G1). Until he meets Tom
Drum, he is an outcast; but the common man does not require a code
of behavior as demanding as that of the life of a noble courtier.[91]
Unlike the nobleman, a shoemaker always has a social and economic
place if he wants it.

A second Shakespearean analogue is seen in the troubles faced by Sir
John Rainsford. When Rainsford loses his temper at the inhumane
priest and buries him alive, he is more like the noble Hotspur than like
Sir John Falstaff. Like both Hotspur and Falstaff, however, the impet-
uous knight finds himself out of favor with the King, and he is forced
to flee in disguise to escape arrest. But though he is in disgrace with
the King, he is welcomed by the shoemakers of London, where he lives
and prospers.

While Deloney's shoemakers, and his craftsmen generally, require
conformity to a code of conduct, the members of "the gentle craft" are
of diverse sorts, interests, and personalities. In the world of courtly politics, a man like Tom Drum, who consistently promises more than he
can deliver and who loves a jest in any circumstance, would have been
banished, as he was given "Tom Drum's entertainment" at the house
of Mistress Farmer. Falstaff, who cannot give up his jests even on the
battlefield, who pragmatically hides from battle and stabs the dead

Hotspur in the thigh so as to be able to affect heroism, is banished because he cannot conform to the role of the nobleman.[92] Tom Drum, who also loves to jest and who attributes "other mens deeds to himselfe" in battle, is welcomed back to his workbench by his fellows. They know "his daily vaunts," but there is room for diversity in "the gentle craft." For all his bragging, Tom Drum is a proud member of the guild. He never does anything to damage the security of the commonwealth.

CHAPTER 4

Thomas Deloney's Reputation

I Deloney's Early Reputation

THOMAS Deloney came upon the literary scene quietly and unnoticed. His first work, a translation from the Latin of "A Declaration Made by the Archbishop of Collen," received no known response. He did attract critical comment when, as a silk weaver, he began to write popular ballads in about 1586. By 1592 he was well known enough in "the yarking up of Ballades" to attract the attention of Robert Greene and Gabriel Harvey, both of whom condemned him as a common balladmonger. Other contemporary writers slandered ballad writers generally and Deloney specifically, street ballads not being much admired by those who chose to refer to them in print. The contemporary remark closest to complimenting Deloney as a balladeer came from Will Kemp, who added a note addressed to "the impudent generation of Balladmakers" to his *Nine Daies Wonder* (April 1600). Suggesting that balladmongers were so disreputable that they would doubtless be tumbled unceremoniously into sinners' graves at their deaths, he reported that Deloney, the "late general" of the balladmongers, had received an honest burial.[1]

Greene's condemnation of Deloney was used partly to promote his own work, but he clearly did not like Deloney's poetry any more than Harvey did. Nashe, on the other hand, was relatively kind to Deloney. Perhaps Nashe's defense of Deloney was nothing more than another weapon to use in his quarrel with Harvey, that long war of words which gives modern readers more of a view of Nashe's love of invective than of his ideas on any particular subject. Nashe may, however, have seen in Deloney's works a style that he more affected than any he found in the other University Wits. Deloney's writings were shocking enough to land him in jail at least once and have his freedom threatened another time. His ballads, recounting as they often did the realistic, sometimes sensational events of the day, must surely have appealed to Nashe, who admitted in the Epistle to *Lenten Stuff* (1599)

118

that his greatest mentor in matters of style was Pietro Aretino (1492–1556). Aretino, who shocked his audiences with gross flattery, libel, and pornography, is said by C. S. Lewis to have been "the yellow press of his day."[2] In Deloney, Nashe may have found a new mentor; for not only was Nashe, like Deloney, persecuted by London authorities who were offended by his works, but he also wrote a work on the destruction of Jerusalem, *Christs Teares ouer Ierusalem* (1593), on the same subject as Deloney's *Canaans Calamatie*.[3] But perhaps the clearest reason Nashe did not join his contemporaries in condemning Deloney is that there was no profit in it for a commercial writer. Much better to attack the respectable Gabriel Harvey, who as Gilgilis Hobberdehoy, Braggadocio Glorioso, Timothy Tiptoes, or Gerboduck Huddleduddle is defenseless. When Nashe chided Harvey for being the son of a ropemaker, Harvey's embarrassment made him the more vulnerable. Call Deloney a silk weaver and he is proud of it. As Nashe says, "had I a Ropemaker to my father and somebody had cast it in my teeth, I would foorthwith haue writ in praise of Ropemakers and prou'd it by sound sillogistry to be one of the 7 liberal sciences."[4] What Deloney did in his works, and profitably too, was to praise clothiers and shoemakers (and craftsmen generally) and prove them to be as valuable to England as any nobleman.

Robert Greene's condemnation of Deloney, one could argue, may have been more stylized than real. The narrator in "Defense of Conny-Catching" is supposedly Cuthbert Cunny-catcher, who complains that his business has been hurt by "R. G." Cuthbert says that Greene has written much insignificant stuff which "had better seemed T. D." instead of addressing himself to the more important work of exposing deceitful parasites in English society. A stronger advertisement for Greene's own work could hardly be imagined. But Cuthbert's complaints about the insignificance of Deloney's ballads reflect, I believe, Greene's own views. Greene was, like Deloney, a commercial writer, but as his Epistle to the *Mourning Garment* (1596) and *Repentance* (1592) show, Greene was concerned about the moral significance of literature, and in the *Vision* (1592) he promises to devote himself to moral and natural philosophy. Like Deloney, Greene was from Norwich, but he would not produce "triviall trinkets and threedbare trash."

Such published criticism does not, however, accurately reflect Deloney's early reputation. Street ballads of the sixteenth century were overly plentiful; they were written in every conceivable style and on every possible subject. "Indeed," Hyder Rollins says, "scarce a cat could look out of a gutter" but some "proper new ballet of a strange sight" would be written.[5] Deloney, being the "general" of the late six-teenth-century ballad writers, although he did not write of strange pigs and deformed humans, was often tarred with the same brush as those who did. The fact is that Deloney was one of a handful of ballad writers whose works were commercially very successful.[6]

Deloney's popularity as a prose writer was certainly no less than his fame as a ballad writer. The fact that not a single copy of a first edition of any of his four prose works is extant suggests that they were read to tatters. The earliest known edition of *Jack of Newbury* is dated 1619, although the work was registered in 1597. Part 1 of *The Gentle Craft* is entered in the Stationers' Register on October 19, 1597, but the earliest known edition is dated 1637. Both *Thomas of Reading* and Part 2 of *The Gentle Craft* were published prior to Deloney's death in 1600, yet editions of 1612 and 1639 respectively are the earliest known.[7]

The prose works were reprinted many times during the seventeenth and eighteenth centuries. For *Jack of Newbury* there are editions running up to 1775, with at least fifteen editions during the seventeenth century alone.[8] The other works have similar publication records. Deloney was still being published by W. J. Thoms in 1858[9] and *Jack of Newbury* by James O. Halliwell in 1859. *The Gentle Craft* appears to have been Deloney's most popular work, with no fewer than twenty-four editions before 1740.[10] *The Gentle Craft* was still being published during the times of Dickens and Thackeray. Alexis Lange notes that the last complete edition of *The Gentle Craft* appeared six years after *Robinson Crusoe* was published.[11]

Deloney's works also proved attractive to other writers as sources. Almost immediately after *The Gentle Craft* was published, it apparently caught the eye of the dramatist Thomas Dekker, who used it as a source for *The Shoemakers' Holiday*. Dekker uses primarily the episode of Simon Eyre in Part 1 of Deloney's work for his plot, but the other two episodes in Part 1 provide suggestions for Dekker's characters. Several other seventeenth-century plays and novels rely partly or wholly upon *The Gentle Craft*, *Jack of Newbury*, and *Thomas of Reading*. Ole Reuter calls attention to a novel by Henry Roberts published in 1600 entitled *Haigh for Devonshire: A pleasant Discourse of six Gallant Marchants of Devonshire, Their Liues, Aduentures, and Trauailes: with sundrie their rare showes and pastimes shewed before *the King in Exeter*. Roberts's work, obviously published soon after Deloney's *Thomas of Reading* appeared, is called by Reuter "a downright theft."[12]

Haigh for Devonshire is a series of episodes concerning William, Robert, Otho, Oliver, John, and Walter, the "sixe Gallant Marchants of Devonshire." The similarity of the structure of this work to that of Deloney's "Sixe Worthy Yeomen of the West" is clear and probably cause enough to justify Reuter's charge. Just as Deloney describes his clothiers as close friends and tells of their traveling, gaming, and eating together, Roberts's episodes describe his merchants as inseparable friends who travel over England, France, and Spain seeking fortune and adventure. But if Roberts borrows the general structure of Deloney's novels, he cannot approach Deloney's skill in creating characters and realistic dialogue. His characters, for example, are indistinguishable from each other in thought, action, or speech. Indeed, there is little dialogue in the novel at all, most of the speeches being reported indirectly. Instead of the idiomatic English of Deloney's Thomas Cole, the broad dialect of Hodgekins, the rich street language of Joan, and the elegant language of the lovers Margaret and Duke Robert, the characters in Henry Roberts's work have no language of their own.

When, for example, Duke Robert woos Margaret, he uses balanced phrases, contrast, alliteration, emotive words, and logic. When Margaret accepts his love, she knows exactly what is being offered:

"Faire Maide, I did long since manifest my loue to thee by my letter; tell me therefore, were it not better to be a Dutches than a drudge? a Lady of high reputation, than a seruant of simple degree? with me thou mightest liue in pleasure, where here thou drawest thy daies forth in paine; by my loue thou shouldst be made a Lady of great treasures: where now thou art poore and beggarly: all manner of delights should then attend on thee, and whatsoeuer thy heart desireth, thou shouldst haue: wherefore seeing it lies in thy owne choice, make thy selfe happy, by consenting to my suite."

(p. 250; sig. G1)

On the other hand, when Roberts's character William woos a wife, the dialogue is reported indirectly, not illustrated:

William being a bashful young man, after many friuolous questions, fearing to be counted a coward hauing such advantage, solicites her for loue, with such pretie questions, and her wittie answeres, that William, after the first assault became valiant, whetting his wittes to answer her parley, wherein he so preuailed that the skirmish waring faint, his hope was the greater to scale the forte without more danger, and like a conquerer might vaunt with honor, the Towne is his, though with some faint denialls, for modestie she said nay, yet upon conditions, her father said Amen. Ioane writes Content.

                                                                                                    (Sig. D2)

The fact that the early editions of Deloney's novels were literally read out of existence and were reprinted in quarto form well into the eighteenth century, along with the evidence that dramatists and other writers of the time borrowed his plots and characters and emulated the structure of his works, show that Deloney enjoyed a wide and appreciative audience during and immediately following his lifetime. The published comments of Kemp, Greene, Nashe, and others, therefore, do not seem to represent fairly his early reputation.

II   *Deloney's Modern Reputation*

If Deloney's audiences read and imitated the prose works with immediate enthusiasm, literary historians have less quickly turned their attention to Deloney either as a poet or prose writer. Many late eighteenth- and early twentieth-century books dealing with the history of the English novel either give Deloney brief mention or, usually, ignore him completely. Wilbur L. Cross (1899) mentions his use of middle-class characters, but Cross is more interested in Deloney as a curiosity than as a contributor to the development of the novel.[13] Neither J. J. Jusserand (1890), Walter Raleigh (1894), F. A. Stoddart (1900), nor George Saintsbury (1913) even mentions Deloney.[14]

The twentieth century, however, has seen a growing popularity of Deloney among critics and literary historians. Ole Reuter finds it remarkable that Deloney has "changed in literary opinion from hardly more than a minor character in an underplot to something of a hero in the history of the English novel."[15] F. W. Chandler praises Deloney not only for contributing to English prose a new type of fiction which analyzes heroes of the people, but also for creating interesting stories and characters.[16] In the most ambitious survey to date of the English novel, Ernest A. Baker devotes a full chapter to Deloney's substantial contributions in bringing realism to English fiction.[17]

With the publication in 1912 by F. O. Mann of the collected works came an increasing interest in Deloney's works, especially his prose. Hyder Rollins, whose work on street ballads acquainted him with

Deloney's poetry directly rather than from contemporary references, calls Deloney a "distinguished" writer as a balladeer.[18] Rollins also contributed two articles on the sources of euphuism in Deloney's prose.[19] In 1926 Abel Chevalley, a great admirer of Deloney, published a thorough study of the economic situation in England about which Deloney wrote in his novels.[20] In 1933 Llewelyn Powys announced, "In all English literature no writer has been more neglected than Thomas Deloney."[21] To Powys, Deloney is an "astonishing genius" and a "great Elizabethan novelist."[22] While Powy's excitement causes him to make excessive statements, he is no more excessive than those critics who would ignore Deloney entirely. Charles Dunn in 1936 is hardly less complimentary than Powys, saying that Deloney's novels "now bring him a firm friend in every reader."[23] Ole Reuter's thorough discussion in 1939 of Deloney's prose style places Deloney in "the front rank of Elizabethan writers."[24]

The publication in 1961 of the prose works by Merritt E. Lawlis is evidence of the continued interest in Deloney. Lawlis shows that Deloney's "fresh and exciting" prose is modeled neither on the romances of Sidney and Lodge, the euphuism of Lyly, nor the underworld realism of Greene and Nashe, but upon the jest book and the drama. So well does Deloney use the best elements of drama, according to Lawlis, that "On his own ground Deloney compares favorably with the best English novelists of the eighteenth and nineteenth centuries. Who besides Dickens is his superior in drawing flat characters?"[25] The key phrase here is, of course, "on his own ground." Deloney's prose works are less polished than most eighteenth- and nineteenth-century novels, but his creation of interesting, individualized characters shows that he is a worthy forerunner to Dickens.

As the creator of the novel of everyday life Deloney has progressed from being condemned by critics, to being ignored, to being recognized as a significant contributor to the history of prose fiction. In recent years his works have received increasing attention as modern scholars have become aware of his considerable abilities in characterization, development of plot, and use of imagery and language. Mann believes that in the works of Deloney "we may justly find the highest achievement of the Elizabethan novel."[26] And while few critics are willing to praise Deloney's works as broadly as Mann is, modern scholarship nevertheless consistently accords Deloney his rightful place in the history of English prose fiction as an artist who set new and important trends in prose.

III   *Deloney's Place in the History of Prose Fiction*

Early English prose had the same origins as poetry and drama: The people's desire to hear stories. English literary history is full of tales of battles, of love, of adventures, of horror, of domestic life, but always tales which, as Sir Philip Sidney said, hold children from play and old men from the chimney corner. The stories of Robin Hood, Bevis of Hampton, Troilus and Criseyde, King Arthur, the wife of Bath, and assorted carpenters and clerks, priests and priors, tailors and tradesmen taught and delighted succeeding generations of Englishmen. The titles of narrative ballads, which entertained a majority of the English population, fill the pages of the Stationers' Register.

The popular stories prior to the sixteenth century were generally in verse, and nothing remotely resembling a novel existed. Prior to the use of the printing press, stories were most often declaimed, and poetry's devices for catching the ear—rhyme, rhythm, alliteration, repetition—were important to the storyteller. Since for centuries the usual medium for stories was verse, a strong tradition insinuated itself so that "literature" was often taken to mean "poetry."[27] The sixteenth-century attack by the Puritans against literature, including drama, drew defenses or apologies for poetry. When Renaissance drama developed out of the divine mating of classical Greek and Roman drama with native English mystery and morality plays, poetry dominated the dialogue. Both *Ralph Roister Doister* and *Gammer Gurtons Needle* distract a modern audience from the plot and characters by the use of couplets in long narratives. Even *Gorboduc*, which uses the more natural blank verse, lulls an audience to sleep with the repetition of over seventeen–hundred lines of strict iambic pentameter.

So strong was the tradition and prestige of poetry that even as the tales grew longer, more complex, and sometimes more realistic than the earlier stories of our culture, verse persisted. But the use of verse in the longer works was not successful, and writers turned to prose, a form less artificial and better suited for the requirements of complex stories. Shakespeare's most successful plays are those that suit the right form—either rhymed verse, blank verse, or prose—to the situation. In *1 Henry IV*, for example, when Prince Hal seeks to establish himself as a majestic, orderly prince, his speech is disciplined and formal, and in verse. When, however, he is playing his political games with Falstaff and the others, he speaks in prose.

Often the experiments with prose in fiction show the same kind of mixture of poetry and prose. George Gascoigne's *Master F. J.* (1573) sprinkles sonnets throughout the prose narrative, as though the author is anxious to protect the value of his work by setting jewels of poetry among the coarser prose. Thomas Lodge, Sir Philip Sidney, and Thomas Deloney also mingle poetry with prose narrative. And John Lyly's *Euphues: An Anatomy of Wit* (1578), with its alliteration, assonance, repetition, and other auditory elements, is surely a blend of poetry and prose.

The subject matter of early prose fiction also closely resembles that of narrative verse. The stories of brave heroes and beautiful mistresses fill the lines of medieval verses in French, German, and English. The courtly love affairs of such characters as Troilus and Criseyde, so popular in verse, were no less popular in prose. Master F. J., in Gascoigne's excellent early novel, falls in love with the coquettish Dame Elinor and suffers from the same courtly lover's maladies as Troilus did. John Lyly's *Euphues: An Anatomy of Wit* presents a romance of language no more realistic than the courtly games played by the knights and ladies of the medieval romances. Even its plot, what little there is of it, concerns the kindnesses and cruelties of women, the transitory nature of love, and the superiority of friendships, all subjects to be found in early verse romances. Sir Philip Sidney's *Arcadia* (1580), although it turned away from the anatomy of wit and muted the euphuistic style, is still a story of romance, not of everyday life. The location of Arcadia changes in Robert Greene's *Pandosto* (1588) and Thomas Lodge's *Rosalind* (1590), but the game is the same: young lovers face hardship and separation, they lose themselves in a pastoral setting, and they resolve their complications and live happily ever after.

No one should underestimate the contribution to English prose fiction made by Lyly, Sidney, Greene, and Lodge. Many modern readers find Lyly's *Euphues* tedious and almost unreadable because of its preoccupation with alliteration, antithesis, use of elaborate similes, and reference to catalogues of fictitious authority to support insignificant arguments. Lyly's style, as Richard Lanham says, "rides over context like a steam roller."[28] But Lyly's work is nevertheless a landmark in the history of English prose fiction, setting a standard that showed the age that English prose was capable of art and grace. Shakespeare mocked the excesses of the euphuistic style, but his best works show the devotion to style, to the careful use of specific language and appropriate imagery, that Lyly designed. Excessive as Lyly's rhetoric was, he illustrated the richness of English. As insignificant as his story was, he at least dealt with ideas in prose fiction. Sidney, Greene, and Lodge were strongly influenced by Lyly, as can be seen by their choices of plots, themes, and styles. They began the modification of Lyly's excessive ornamentation, carrying a popular new style a step further toward a more natural method of telling a story. The style is still affected, but less so than Lyly's. The stories are still tied to the pastoral romance, but there is more characterization and more action.

Thomas Nashe's *Jack Wilton, or the Unfortunate Traveller* (1594) marks something of a departure from the long tradition of romance in English literature. Here realism, exaggerated as in the jest books, displaces romance in plot, character, and setting. Nashe is like a journalist, reporting through Jack Wilton the seamy side of Elizabethan life. In his adventures, Jack wanders from England through Europe and back to France commenting upon people, places, and events. His description of the rape of Heraclide and the torture of Zadoch are so far from the generally pleasant scenes described in the pastoral romances as to be anti-romance. Ernest A. Baker argues that, as a predecessor of Daniel Defoe, Nashe wanted to show "that real life, as men saw it or read about it in the current narratives of travellers and historians, was as rich in savour and as wildly exciting as the lawless invention of the romancers."[29] Although Nashe's parody of romance is as weak in plot and psychological character development as the earlier prose works, he does offer anti-romantic incidents, exaggerated though they be, as the subject matter of his work.

It was Thomas Deloney, however, who settled the subject matter of prose fiction quite naturally into the homes, shops, and everyday lives of middle-class people. Deloney borrowed anecdotes from the jest books, stories of chivalry from medieval romances, and occasionally even the language of *Euphues*. But always the essential element of Deloney's prose works is the life of the clothier or shoemaker in a utopian commonwealth. Deloney finds his heroes not among kings and queens, although characters of royal and noble blood appear in his description of English life. Deloney's heroes are John Winchcombe, Thomas Cole, Simon Eyre, Richard Casteler, Master Peachey, and other competent, hard-working craftsmen who defend God and country while producing clothing or boots of quality. The problems his most memorable characters face are usually the realistic problems of the shop, the house, and the street; his settings are always an ideal state where his worthy craftsmen can achieve social and economic success. Certainly the homiletic tradition did not cease when the Renaissance began, and Deloney's poetry and prose generally are in the line of didactic English literature, the main purpose of which was to instruct its readers in right living. But his characters are not the stereotyped embodiments of vice and virtue. Baker is of the opinion that "when we turn to character-drawing, neither Lyly nor Sidney, not even Nashe, with his fierce portraits in the malevolent style of a lampoon, has a leg to stand on in comparison with Deloney."[30]

Deloney's middle-class origins; his intimate knowledge of the problems, dreams, and strengths of common men and women; his sense of realism and humor; his love of language and literary devices; his narrative skill; his native perception; and his devotion to justice, order, and pragmatism combine to result in something new in English prose. His literary sources are the jest books, *novelle*, chronicle histories, romances, and dramas. But his major source is the middle-class Elizabethan from whom Deloney takes his dialogue, characters, settings, moods, and themes. Tradition and his individual talent and experience serve him better than Lyly, Sidney, Greene, or even Nashe as models for his art. Deloney's value as a writer of prose fiction and his importance in the history of the genre are based in this hearty realism and in his creation of a model commonwealth which merges the traditional order and obedience of the medieval hierarchy with a new democracy which encouraged social and economic mobility. He writes of industrious tradesmen, like Jack of Newbury and Thomas of Reading. His female characters are sometimes witty, like Mrs. Eyre and Jack's widow; sometimes babbling, like Mrs. Winchcombe's gossip and Sutton's wife. He presents buffoons, like Will Sommers, Tom Drum, and Round Robin. He tells of foolish lovers, like Master Benedick and Cutbert. But in every case his characters and atmosphere are drawn from life. One looks in vain for such unprepossessing realism in other prose works of the time.

The emergence of the middle-class hero as the protagonist in novels reflects the changing social and economic system in England and the world; indeed, Deloney's works generally appear to owe their existence to the economic pressures caused by what L. C. Knights calls "the double aspect of the age ('medieval' and 'modern'),"[31] the development of capitalistic enterprise in an essentially communal system. New markets abroad and the discover of immense wealth in the form of Spanish and American gold created the realistic chance that a middle-class citizen could, by wise investment, hard work, and good luck, become rich. But the new economic system also brought with it ills against which the community-based economic system had protected the workers: inflation and unemployment. Into this brave new world of opportunity and danger Deloney sends his heroes to seek their ways. L. C. Knights remarks that while Elizabethan drama refers to the social and economic problems of the day, "None of them, we notice, is a dramatization of an economic problem or consciously intended as propaganda for this or that form of economic organization, and only a few of them ... are meant to make the audience think about questions of social morality."[32] Deloney's works, however, especially the novels, are clearly "intended as propaganda" for a particular form of economic organization.

The economic system Deloney's characters consistently argue for is neither the restricted community-based economy nor the exciting but dangerous new capitalism; it is a blend of the two. Deloney's heroes are capitalists; they seek wealth, and when they are good enough business men and women, they attain it. But in his model commonwealth Deloney's heroes who attain wealth never turn their backs upon their fellows who are in need. The rulers of Jerusalem who disdained the needs of the community in order selfishly to provide for their own desires are plainly cast as villains by Deloney in *Canaans Calamitie*. Indeed, their failure to be concerned for the common citizen, especially for Miriam and her son, brings about their doom. Jack of Newbury rises to a position of power and enjoys great wealth, but his life is spent using that power and wealth to support his community, as did the historical John Winchcombe, whose talents and largess endeared him to succeeding generations of Newbury residents. Thomas of Reading spends his life in service to his community and to England. On the night of his death he provides money for his fellow clothier, Thomas Dove, who would otherwise have gone to debtor's prison. Simon Eyre, fortunate and shrewd enough to attain wealth and position, believes that it is necessary that he use his means to benefit others: "seeing God hath bestowed vpon me that I neuer looked for; it is reason that I should perform my promise [to provide breakfast for all apprentice shoemakers in London]" (p. 132; sig. I3v). His wife agrees: "wherefore sendeth God goods, but therewithall to do him and your Countrey seruice?" (p. 122; sig. H2). Richard Casteler, Lusty Peachey, the Green King—the list of craftsmen heroes is long. They all prosper as capitalists, and they all support the community as the foundation of their social and economic lives. Deloney, standing on the threshold of the modern world, saw the realistic problems of that world clearly, if simplistically; and he drew characters from history and legend and situations from his own imagination to solve those problems.[33]

Deloney's literary reputation does not, however, rest exclusively upon his contribution of realism to prose fiction. While his novels do not show the polish of modern novels, his works nevertheless are artistic and successful as prototypes. Deloney pays close attention to matters of characterization, imagery, and language. He does not probe the motives of his characters, but they are nevertheless captivating characters, made so by Deloney's ability to present the essential and individual trait of each through dramatic means. Cutbert's love of women, Tom Dove's devotion to music, Simon's desire for pottage, Randoll Pert's fate to be both pathetic and burlesque, Long Meg's wit, Simon Eyre's simple devotion to his wife: all of Deloney's characters are individual and memorable. The imagery he uses is drawn generally from the weather, the elements, plants, and animals; like his characters, the imagery is from phenomena common and familiar to middle- and lower-class Englishmen. As for his language, Deloney experiments with euphuism, dialect, and even the slurred speech of drunks. But for the most part, his prose is the vigorous, idiomatic language of daily middle-class Elizabethan life, a language spoken by royalty, nobility, and craftsman alike.

Deloney's characters are interesting people who are full of life; his imagery is clear, appropriate, and fresh; and his love of and ability to use language is demonstrated in his works, even in some of the ballads of his apprenticeship days. Deloney was a perceptive writer who analyzed the main currents of everyday life and created fiction from it with consistent craftsmanship. In the history of English prose fiction Deloney was the first to treat seriously the lives of common people. As a writer of fiction, he precedes Defoe as the creator of the prototype of the modern novel. His stories, settings, characters, language, and imagery are from the life he observed, and they are believable and significant.

Notes and References

Chapter One

1. Louis B. Wright, *Middle-Class Culture in Elizabethan England* (Chapel Hill, 1935), p. 1.
2. Both F. P. Wilson, "The English Jestbooks of the Sixteenth and Early Seventeenth Centuries," *Huntington Library Quarterly*, 2(1939), 143, and J. Woodrow Hassell, Jr., "An Elizabethan Translation of the Tales of Des Périers: *The Mirrour of Mirth*, 1583 and 1592," *Studies in Philology*, 52(1955), 172–85, credit Deloney with the translation.
3. See Merritt Lawlis, *The Novels of Thomas Deloney* (Bloomington, Indiana, 1961), pp. xxiv-xxv, on this subject. Hereafter this will be cited as Lawlis, *Novels*.
4. Will Kemp, *Kemps Nine Daies Wonder*, ed. G. B. Harrison (London, The Bodley Head, 1923), p. 20 (London, 1600, sig. D3v).
5. See the *Dictionary of National Biography*.
6. Lawlis, *Novels*, p. xxiii.
7. Mann, *The Works of Thomas Deloney* (Oxford, 1912), p. vii.
8. Nashe calls Deloney "the Balletting Silke Weaver" ("Have with you to Saffron-Walden," *The Works of Thomas Nashe*, ed. Ronald B. McKerrow [London, 1904–10], III, 84 [London, 1596, sig. N3]), but Mann misquotes Nashe as referring to Deloney as "the Balletting Silke Weaver of Norwich" (see Mann, p. [vii]).
9. "Deloney" is probably a variant of the French name "Delaunay" or "De l'Aunay." Aunay is a town in Brittany in northwestern France. (I am indebted to my colleague Professor Arthur Gionet for this suggestion.)
10. John Stow, *A Survey of the Cities of London and Westminster, Brought Down from the Year 1633 to the Present Time*, ed. John Strype (London, 1720), p. 233.
11. Wright, p. 48.
12. Wright, p. 48.
13. See G. W. Kuehn, "Thomas Deloney: Two Notes," *Modern Language Notes* 52(1937), 103.
14. Kuehn, p. 103.
15. Nashe, III, 84 (sig. N3).
16. Gabriel Harvey, "Pierce's Supererogation," *The Works of Gabriel Harvey, DCL.* ed. Alexander B. Grosart (London, 1844–85), II, 281 (London, 1593, p. 184).
17. Robert Greene, "The Defense of Conny-Catching," *The Works of*

Robert Greene, ed. Alexander B. Grosart (London, 1881–86), XI, 49–50 (London, 1591, sig. B2).

18. See Frances Consitt, *The London Weavers' Company* (Oxford, 1933), I, 146–47; 312–18.

19. Stow, II, 280–81.

20. Kemp, p. 20 (sig. D3v).

21. Kemp, p. 21 (sig D3v).

Chapter Two

1. Richard Sievers categorizes the three types of ballads as "die volksballaden," "Kunstballaden," and "straβenballaden." See "Thomas Deloney: Eine Studie über Balladenlitterature der Shakespere Zeit," *Palaestra,* 36 (1904), 130.

2. This and all subsequent references to the works of Deloney are from *The Works of Thomas Deloney,* ed. F. O. Mann (Oxford, 1912). Listed second are notes to early quartos as follows: (CC) *Canaans Calamitie, or the Dolefull destruction of faire Ierusalem* (London, 1618); (SH) *Strange Histories, of Kings, Princes, Dukes, Earles, Lords, Ladies, Knights, and Gentlemen* (London, 1602); (GGW) *The Garland of Good Will* (London, 1631); *The Pleasant Historie of Iohn Winchcomb, in younger yeares called Iack of Newbery* (London, 1626); *Thomas of Reading, or the sixe worthie yeomen of the west* (London, 1623); *The Gentle Craft* (London, 1648); and *The Gentle Craft, The second Part* (London, 1639). References to miscellaneous ballads (MB) are from various individual, often unique, copies. For a list of extant miscellaneous ballads by Deloney, see Mann, pp. 595–600.

3. Roger Ascham, "The Scholemaster," *Elizabethan Critical Essays,* ed. Gregory Smith (London, 1904), I, 31 (London, 1570, p. 60v).

4. Thomas Lodge, "Defense of Poetry," *Elizabethan Critical Essays,* I, 76 (London, 1579–80, p. 20).

5. William Webbe, "A Discourse of English Poetrie," *Elizabethan Critical Essays,* I, 229 (London, 1586, sigs. C3-C3v).

6. As, for example, the "O" added to every fourth line of the folk ballad "Edward."

7. Webbe, p. 246 (sigs. D1-D1v).

8. Albert Friedman, *The Viking Book of Folk Ballads of the English-Speaking World* (New York, 1956), p. xxvii. Friedman goes on to describe the broadsides as "drenched in sentimentality; cheap pathos mars many of them; a tawdry optimism based on conventional piety and material coziness suffuses the lot."

9. Hyder E. Rollins, *An Analytical Index to the Ballad-Entries (1557–1709) in the Registers of the Company of Stationers of London* (Chapel Hill, 1924). Rollins records such titles as "A cart load of cuckolds whoe are to bee conveyed to Cuckaldo haven," "A combat betwene a man and his wife

for the breches," "The Cramp in my Knee," "A Strange and monstruous fishe seene in the sea on friday the 17 of february 1603," and "A Strange Relacion of a female Monster."

10. See Mann, pp. 495–503.

11. See Kuehn, p. 104.

12. Mann, pp. 495–503.

13. Mann, pp. 503–505.

14. Mann, p. 585.

15. Hyder E. Rollins, "The Black-Letter Broadside Ballad," *PMLA*, 34 (1919), 297.

16. Rollins, "The Black-Letter Broadside Ballad," p. 297.

17. Ritson, *Ancient Songs and Ballads* (London, 1877), p. lxxxv.

18. Gummere, *The Popular Ballad* (Boston, 1907), p. 12.

19. See Gummere, p. 12; Sievers, p. 212; Mann. p. xxxvi. Of "Fair Flower of Northumberland" Sievers says, "Fraglos haben wir es hier mit einer echten Volksball. aus dem Norden zu tun" (p. 121).

20. See Mann, p. xxvii.

21. Deloney's use of specific detail and first-person narration suggest to F. O. Mann that "Deloney himself may have taken part in the Spanish expedition" (p. 581). The fact that another ballad, "The Spanish Lady's Love to an English Gentlemen," deals with certain aspects of the English occupation of Spain might lend credence to Mann's thoughts. But there are no details in any of these poems that could not have been generally known in England. Insofar as Deloney's use of first person is concerned, he is as adaptable as any poet who ever lived in using varied personae: soldiers, sailors, historical characters, women, and in one case, in "The Lamentation of Beccles" (MB. p. 457), he even uses a town as persona.

22. "The Miraculous victory . . . ," *Elizabethan Backgrounds*, ed. Arthur F. Kinney (Hamden, Connecticut, 1975), p. 257 (sig. Ddd5v).

23. J. O. Halliwell, ed. "Early Naval Ballads of England," *Early English Poetry, Ballads, and Popular Literature of the Middle Ages* (London, 1840), II, 18.

24. The other seven ballads that use dialogue extensively are "An English Merchant Born in Chichester," "The Death of Rosamond," "The Banishment of Two Dukes," "The Noble Acts of Arthur of the Round Table," "Of a Prince of England, who wooed the kings daughter of France," "King Edward the third," and "How Couentry was made Free."

25. Mann, p. xxxvi.

26. Mann, p. xxxiv.

27. Mann, p. xxxviii.

28. Mann, p. 600.

29. See Mann, p. 599.

30. It is interesting to note that C. S. Lewis condemns Samuel Daniel's "Complaint of Rosamond" and, by implication, all historical poetry by saying, "But we have learned to expect the worst from any descendant of the

Mirror for Magistrates" (*English Literature in the Sixteenth Century* [Oxford, 1954], p. 526).

31. Professor Tucker Brooke and others regularly assume that *Canaans Calamitie* was written by Thomas Dekker merely because the initials "T. D." appear on the title page (see *A Literary History of England,* ed. Albert C. Baugh [New York, 1948], p. 441). F. O. Mann, however, argues convincingly that "T. D." refers to Thomas Deloney, not Thomas Dekker (see Mann, pp. 593–94).

32. Thomas Nashe, *Christs Teares ouer Ierusalem, Works of Thomas Nashe,* ed. R. B. McKerrow (London, 1904), II, 15 (sig. A1).

33. C. S. Lewis, pp. 410–11.

34. Nashe, p. 71 (sig. I1).

35. Nashe, p. 75 (sig. I3v).

36. Nashe may have altered his style because he was sincerely sorry that he had wasted his life writing satire. He says in his "To the Reader," "In those vaines heere-to-fore haue I mispent my spirite, and prodigally conspir'd against good houres" (*Christs Teares,* p. 12; sig. °3v). More likely, however, since he later wrote *The Unfortunate Traveler,* he was trying to win the favor of Lady Elizabeth Carey, to whom the work is dedicated.

37. Sir William J. Ashley, *An Introduction to English Economic History and Theory* (London, 1888), I, 76.

38. I shall detail the important economic problems of the late sixteenth century in the next chapter.

39. Greene, "Quippe for an Upstart Courtier," X, 209 (London, 1592, sig. C2).

40. See Peter Clark and Paul Slack, *English Towns in Transition* (London, 1976), p. 93.

Chapter Three

1. Mann, p. xi.

2. Ashley, *Introduction to English Economic History and Theory,* II, 168.

3. William Cunningham, *The Growth of English Industry and Commerce, The Middle Ages* (Cambridge, England, 1905), I, 464.

4. Peter Clark and Paul Slack report that some economic variations occurred, especially among larger communities. See *English Towns in Transition, 1500–1700* (London, 1976), p. 112.

5. L. C. Knights, *Drama and Society in the Age of Jonson* (London, 1937), p.33.

6. Astrid Friis, *Alderman Cockayne's Project and the Cloth Trade: The Commercial Policy of England in its Main Aspects, 1603–1625* (London 1927), p. 12.

7. *Acts of the Privy Council: James I (1616–1617)*, ed. John Roche Dasent (London, 1927), XXXV, 20.

8. Friis, p. 61.

9. Knights, p. 122.

10. Peter Ramsey believes that although English privateers were able to make some "lucky hauls" of Spanish silver, not enough of the bullion was introduced into England to be the "mainspring" of inflation in sixteenth-century England. See his *Tudor Economic Problems* (London, 1963), pp. 116–17. Earl Hamilton's study of the Spanish price revolution shows the great impact American treasure had on prices in Andalusia from 1503 to 1660. How seriously American gold and silver affected the English economy is another question. See "American Treasure and Andalusian Prices, 1503–1660," *The Price Revolution in Sixteenth-Century England*, ed. Peter H. Ramsey (London, 1971), pp. 147–81.

11. J. M. Keynes, *A Treatise on Money* (New York, 1930), II, 156–57.

12. Knights, p. 55.

13. Knights, p. 134.

14. William R. Scott, *The Constitution and Finance of English, Scottish, and Irish Joint-Stock Companies to 1720* (Cambridge, England, 1910–12) I, 100.

15. See Peter Ramsey, *Tudor Economic Problems*, pp. 20–22; 26–29; 32–36.

16. Francis Abernathy has found four particular social problems discussed in the popular literature of the fifteenth and sixteenth centuries: religion and reformation, rogues and vagabonds, inflation, and enclosure. See "Popular Literature and Social Protest, 1485–1558," *Studies in English Renaissance Literature*, ed. Waldo McNeir (Louisiana Studies, Humanities Series, No. 12 [Baton Rouge, 1962]), pp. 1–19.

17. Peter Ramsey calls wool exports during the fourteenth century "the milch-cow of a needy royal exchequer." *Tudor Economic Problems*, p. 50.

18. See Christopher Hill, *Reformation to Industrial Revolution, 1530–1780* (New York, 1967), p. 73.

19. *The Elizabethan World Picture* (New York, 1944), p. 8.

20. Nashe, "Have with you to Saffron-Walden," III, 84 (sig. N3).

21. For a Study of the economic problems underlying Deloney's works, see Abel Chevalley, *Thomas Deloney: Le Roman des Métiers au Temps de Shakespeare* (Paris, 1926) and Lawrence Stone, *The Causes of the English Revolution, 1529–1642* (London, 1972), especially pp. 47–117.

22. Ian Watt, *The Rise of the Novel* (Berkeley, 1957), pp. 48–49.

23. Northrop Frye, *Anatomy of Criticism* (Princeton, 1975), pp. 304–05.

24. Frye, p. 305.

25. Abel Chevalley believes that Deloney was attempting to mirror reality in his portraits of middle-class life. I believe that Larryetta M. Schall, in an unpublished dissertation in 1972, was the first to point out the utopian nature

of Deloney's fiction. See "The Proletarian Tradition and Thomas Deloney," Diss. University of Nevada, 1972, p. 89.

26. Merritt Lawlis, *Elizabethan Prose Fiction* (New York, 1967), p. 551.

27. Watt, pp. 48–49.

28. Greene, "The Defense of Conny-Catching," XI, 49 (sig. B2).

29. Powys, "Thomas Deloney," *Virginia Quarterly Review*, 9(1933), 578.

30. An exception is Alexis F. Lange, "Thomas of Reading," *Palaestra*, 18(1903), xv-xvi. Will Kemp in *Kemps Nine Daies Wonder*, p. 21 (sig. D4), also lists "the 6 yeomen of the west" first in a list of Deloney's novels, but there was probably no attempt on his part to offer an accurate chronology.

31. Mann, p. 547.

32. Lawlis, *Novels*, p. xxix.

33. See Hyder E. Rollins, "Thomas Deloney's Euphuistic Learning and *The Forest*," *PMLA*, 50(1935), 406.

34. Thomas Fuller, *The Worthies of England*, ed. John Freeman (London, 1952), I, 137 (London, 1662).

35. See Mann, p. xi.

36. Mann, pp. 506–08.

37. Mann, p. 508.

38. "Thomas Deloney and the Virtuous Proletariat," *Cambridge Journal*, 5(1951), 47.

39. *English Towns in Transition, 1500–1700* (London, 1976), p. 125.

40. *The Crisis of the Aristocracy* (Oxford, 1965), p. 30.

41. *The Articulate Citizen and the English Renaissance* (Durham, N.C., 1965), p. 365.

42. This sounds like a traditional proverb, but it does not appear in M. P. Tilley, *A Dictionary of the Proverbs in England in the Sixteenth and Seventeenth Centuries* (Ann Arbor, 1950).

43. James Lee Traylor, in an unpublished dissertation, discusses the thematic relationship which "exists between the lives of the lovers involved in their courtship and marriage relationships and the ideal of the well-ruled state." See "The Thematic Use of Courtship and Marriage in Thomas Deloney's Novels: A Study in the Origins of Realism in Elizabethan Fiction," Diss. Georgia State University, 1977, p. 36.

44. Merritt E. Lawlis describes the Randoll Pert scene as "Chaplinesque" in *Apology for the Middle Class* (Bloomington, Indiana, 1960), p. 95.

45. Baker believes that Deloney is mocking euphuism in the widow's speech, but I see no reason to believe that he is. See *History of the English Novel* (New York, 1924), II, 176.

46. Baker, p. 174.

47. Wright, *Middle-Class Culture*, p. 44.

48. The dominance of animal imagery throughout Deloney's prose works is noted by Margrit Hablützel, *Die Bildwelt Thomas Deloneys* (Bern, 1946), who says, "Weitaus die grösste Gruppe bilden die Tiere," p. 11.

49. In the first chapter alone, other animal images used to define characters are a salamander, herring, sheep, swallow, goose, rabbit, chicken, crab, ass, dog, spider, frog, fly, worm, pelican, and various other birds, beasts, and fish.

50. Lawlis, *Novels*, p. xix.

51. Lawlis, *Novels*, p. xix.

52. The effect of the alliteration, and probably the intent, is metonymic. Gray is Gloucester, Sutton is Salisburie, and so on. So important was clothing to the economy of England that, as the chief clothier of the town, each man would probably have been chief citizen as well.

53. The "authorless pamphlet" is, of course, Deloney's novel.

54. Fuller, *Worthies of England*, I, 137.

55. This and all subsequent references to Holinshed are from *The Chronicles of England, Scotland, and Ireland* (London, 1587).

56. Mann, p. 549.

57. Mann, p. 549.

58. Reginald Scot, *Discoverie of Witchcraft*, ed. Hugh Ross Williamson (Arundel, 1964), p. 301 (London, 1584).

59. Simon's wife displays the kind of greed that Deloney condemns in *Canaans Calamitie* and elsewhere, the acquisitiveness which, as I have shown, infected the new economic order of the late sixteenth century. Deloney describes her as one "wholly bent to pride and pleasure" (p. 233). Simon gives in to her greed, not because he agrees with her, but because he loves her.

60. Wright, *Middle-Class Culture*, p. 367.

61. Ole Reuter, "Some Aspects of Thomas Deloney's Prose Style," *Neuphilologische Mitteilungen*, 40 (1939), 70.

62. Unfortunately no one knows which work was written first. Since both scenes are so integral a part of *Thomas of Reading*, we can assume that they were probably included in the first edition of about 1597, whereas *Macbeth* was probably not written until 1606. The earliest extant edition of *Thomas of Reading*, however, is 1612.

63. Baker, *History of the English Novel*, II, 187.

64. de Voragine Jacobus, *The Golden Legend*, translated by William Caxton ed. F. S. Ellis (London, 1900), VI, 62 (London 1527, p. cclxxxv).

65. Jacobus, VI, 127 (p. ccc).

66. Jacobus, VI, 129 (p. ccc).

67. Tilley, *Dictionary*, p. 582 (S44).

68. Mann, p. 522.

69. Jacobus, VI, 69 (p. cclxxxvii).

70. Mann, p. 523.

71. Deloney's source for this battle is Thomas Johnson's *Cornucopiae* (1595). See Hyder Rollin's "Deloney's Sources for Euphuistic Learning," *PMLA*, 51(1936), 401–02.

72. For a discussion of the decaying aristocracy during the sixteenth and seventeenth centuries, see Lawrence Stone, *The Causes of the English Revolution* (London, 1972), pp. 83–84, 124–25 and *Crisis of the Aristocracy* (Oxford, 1965).

73. It is possible that Deloney is intentionally poking fun at overly romantic characters. Winifred's and Sir Hugh's actions are so extreme and their motivations so slight that they appear ridiculous. Deloney's craftsmen as heroes seldom make such errors.

74. Reuter, "Some Aspects of Thomas Deloney's Prose Style," p. 70.

75. "Thomas Dekker's *Twelfth Night*," *University of Toronto Quarterly*, 41(Fall 1971), 64. See also James H. Conover, *Thomas Dekker: An Analysis of Dramatic Structure* (The Hague, 1969).Conover says that Dekker "purifies" Deloney's Simon Eyre by removing the deception involved in acquiring the goods from the wrecked ship. Dekker's Eyre, however, is more lucky than deserving.

76. Holinshed, II, 1083.

77. Grafton, p. 1323 (II, 531).

78. Holinshed, II, 1083.

79. See Mann, p. 531.

80. Mann, p. 531.

81. Mann, pp. 532–35.

82. Usually Jack or John Drum. See Tilley, p. 344 (J12), and Mann, p. 535.

83. Henry Chettle, *Kind-Hartes Dreame*, ed. G. B. Harrison (London, 1923), p. 12 (London, 1593, sig. B2v).

84. Rollins, "Thomas Deloney's Euphuistic Learning and *The Forest*," *PMLA*, 50(1935), 679–86, and "Deloney's Sources for Euphuistic Learning," *PMLA*, 51(1936), 399–406.

85. Mann, p. 531.

86. Wright, *Middle-Class Culture*, p. 371.

87. Tilley, p. 214 (F255).

88. Mann, p. 537.

89. Tilley, p. 637 (S929).

90. These last three proverbs do not appear in Tilley.

91. Shakespeare suggests the difference in lifestyles in several of his plays. In *As You Like It* the shepherd Corin, for example, is proud of the fact that he is "a true laborer" and not a courtier. He says, "I earn that I eat, get that I wear, owe no man's hate, envy no man's happiness, glad of other men's good, content with my harm, and the greatest of my pride is to see my ewes graze and my lambs suck" (III. ii. 77–81).

92. See my "Hal and Francis in *King Henry IV, Part I:* Another View," *McNeese Review*, 22(1975–76), 62–69.

Chapter Four

1. Kemp, p. 21 (sig. D3v).

2. C. S. Lewis, *English Literature in the Sixteenth Century*, p. 411.

3. Deloney, in this case, is probably using Nashe as a source, although which work was written first is not absolutely certain. Either way, the similarities between the two writers are clear.

4. Thomas Nashe, "Strange News, of the Interception of Certaine Letters," *The Works of Thomas Nashe*, ed. Ronald B. McKerrow (London, 1904–1910, I, 270 (London, 1592, sig. C2v).

5. Rollins, "The Black-Letter Broadside Ballad," p. 266.

6. Rollins, "The Black-Letter Broadside Ballad," p. 297.

7. Kuehn, "Thomas Deloney: Two Notes," p. 105.

8. F. W. Chandler, *The Literature of Roguery* (London, 1907), p. 72.

9. W. J. Thoms, ed., *Collection of Early English Prose Romance* (London, 1858).

10. Arundel J. K. Esdaile, *A List of English Tales and Prose Romances Printed before 1740* (London, 1921), pp. 38–41.

11. Alexis F. Lange, ed., "*The Gentle Craft* by Thomas Deloney," *Palaestra*, 18(1903), p. xxvii.

12. Reuter, "Some Aspects of Thomas Deloney's Prose Style," p. 20.

13. W. L. Cross, *The Development of the English Novel* (New York, 1899), p. 12.

14. J. J. Jusserand, *The English Novel in the Time of Shakespeare*, translated by Elizabeth Lee (London, 1890); Walter Raleigh, *The English Novel* (New York, 1894); F. H. Stoddard, *The Evolution of the English Novel* (New York, 1900); George Saintsbury, *The English Novel* (New York, 1913).

15. Reuter, "Some Aspects of Thomas Deloney's Prose Style," pp. 23–24.

16. Chandler, p. 72.

17. Baker, II, 170–99.

18. Rollins, "The Black-Letter Broadside Ballad," p. 297.

19. "Thomas Deloney's Euphuistic Learning and *The Forest*," *PMLA*, 50(1935), 679–86; "Deloney's Sources for Euphuistic Learning," *PMLA*, 51(1936), 399–406.

20. Abel Chevalley, *Thomas Deloney: Le Roman des Métiers au Temps de Shakespeare* (Paris, 1926).

21. Powys, p. 578.

22. Powys, p. 578.

23. Charles Dunn, "Weaver of Silk, Spinner of Tales," *McMaster University Quarterly*, 45(April 1936), 55.

24. Reuter, "Some Aspects of Thomas Deloney's Prose Style," p. 23.

25. Lawlis, *The Novels*, p. xxiii.

26. Mann, p. xiv.

27. To Sidney, as Walter Davis points out, "poetry" had the broader meaning of "fiction." *Idea and Art in Elizabethan Fiction* (Princeton, 1969), p. 28.

28. Walter Davis and Richard Lanham, *Sidney's Arcadia* (New Haven, 1965), p. 393.

29. Baker, II, 160.

30. Baker, II, 191.

31. Knights, p. 5.

32. Knights, p. 6.

33. Walter Davis is wrong, I believe, in saying that Deloney's fiction differs from chivalric romance "in its reportorial technique—and in nothing else" (*Idea and Art*, p. 269). True, Deloney's heroes exhibit the chivalric values of "piety, patriotism, and thirst for fame," but the context is always the economic, social life of Deloney's day, and the "idealism" of the craftsmen heroes is always a response to reality rather than to romance.

Selected Bibliography

PRIMARY SOURCES

The Novels of Thomas Deloney. Edited by Merrit E. Lawlis. Bloomington: Indiana University Press, 1961. A reprinting of the earliest extant editions of Deloney's four novels, all collated with other editions. The result is a copy of all the best texts, with significant emendations recorded in notes. The Introduction sketches Deloney's life and discusses his use of the jest book and drama as material for his prose works.

The Works of Thomas Deloney. Edited by Francis Oscar Mann. Oxford: The Clarendon Press, 1912. Includes extant prose and poetry, copious notes, explanations, and an introduction. Although succeeding scholars have found extant copies of editions missed by Mann, this collection remains a solid scholarly effort and the only complete collection of Deloney's works.

SECONDARY SOURCES

BAKER, ERNEST A. *The History of the English Novel*. Volume II, "The Elizabethan Age and After." New York: Barnes and Noble, Inc., 1936. A fair, if somewhat limited, discussion of Deloney's novel as occupying "a foremost place in the history of Elizabethan fiction."

CHEVALLEY, ABEL. *The Modern English Novel*, translated from the French by Ben Ray Redman. New York: Alfred A. Knopf, 1925. Sees in Deloney's *Thomas of Reading* the beginnings of realism in English fiction.

————. *Thomas Deloney: le Roman des Métiers au temps de Shakespeare.* Paris: Librairie Gallimard, 1926. Discusses Deloney's novels as both for and about middle-class merchants, unlike all other prose fiction up to his time. Included is a discussion of the economic problems in Elizabethan England which influenced Deloney's works. This is a major study.

CLARK, PETER, and PAUL SLACK, eds. *Crisis and Order in English Towns, 1500–1700*. Toronto: University of Toronto Press, 1972. A collection of essays on various urban areas in England. The essays present information gleaned from public records in an attempt to expand our knowledge of the social and economic history of the period.

————. *English Towns in Transition, 1500–1700*. London: Oxford University Press, 1976. Expands upon the discussion of changes in the urban hierarchy begun in Chapter I of *Crisis and Order* (*supra*). Discusses the

141

economies, social structures, political orders, and cultures of both rural
and urban English towns.

DAVIS, WALTER R. *Idea and Art in Elizabethan Fiction.* Princeton: Princeton
University Press, 1969. Investigates major Elizabethan fiction to determine how it tests "ideas of value by means of experience." The chapter
on "Thomas Deloney and Middle-Class Fiction" summarizes many of
the ideas of Mann and Lawlis, but concludes with the idea that Deloney's "realism" is merely "reportorial"; that is, Davis says that Deloney
describes factual details accurately, but that his view of life is romantic,
not realistic. Chevalley, I believe, is more accurate than Davis in seeing
Deloney's reflection of sixteenth-century economic life as a realism that
was "l'enfance du roman" (Chevalley, p. 133). Davis is not always accurate in reporting plot details.

DORSINVILLE, MAX. "Design in Deloney's *Jack of Newbury.*" *PMLA,* 88
(1973), 233–39. Sees Deloney as an educated man "so conscious of a
distinct socioliterary tradition that he structured a novel on its
inversion."

DUNN, CHARLES W. "Weaver of Silk, Spinner of Tales: A Study of Thomas
Deloney, Novelist." *McMaster University Quarterly,* 45 (1936), 49–55.
A brief and incomplete summary of the novels. Praises Deloney for
being the writer of the common man: "Somewhat of a Red, in other
words!"

HABLÜTZEL, MARGRIT ELISABETH, *Die Bildwelt Thomas Deloneys.* Bern: Ver-
lag A. Francke Ag., 1946. A detailed listing of Deloney's use of imagery
in his prose compared and contrasted with the use of imagery by other
writers of his time. Tables are included to show the types of images used
and their frequency.

HOWARTH, ROBERT GUY. *Two Elizabethan Writers of Fiction: Thomas Nashe
and Thomas Deloney.* Cape Town: The University of Cape Town, 1956.
Discusses Deloney's career as a poet and prose writer. Calls him "The
best of the later Elizabethan novelists."

KNIGHTS, L. C. *Drama and Society in the Age of Jonson.* New York, George
W. Stewart, Inc., 1937. Discusses the effect of the development of the
capitalistic enterprise and accompanying economic problems in six-
teenth- and early seventeenth-century society in England. Knights finds
that literature of the time, especially that of Jonson, reflects a culture
shaped by "perhaps the period of the greatest economic confusion in our
history." Knights, although the questions he asks are significant, is dated;
and his conclusions need to be revised to account for later evidence
found by Peter Ramsey, Lawrence Stone, and others.

KUEHN, G. W. "Thomas Deloney: Two Notes." *Modern Language Notes,* 52
(1937), 103–05. One note points out that F. O. Mann had learned the
birth date of Deloney's son from a copy of the parish register rather than
from the original and had thus copied "weaver" as Deloney's occupation

rather than "silk-weaver" as in the original. The second note locates some seven sixteenth- and seventeenth-century editions of Deloney's novels not mentioned by Mann, some earlier than the copy-texts Mann used.

LAWLIS, MERRITT E. *Apology for the Middle Class*. Bloomington: Indiana University Press, 1960. A thorough but elementary discussion of the realistic dialogue, the plot structure, and characterization of Deloney's novels. Includes plot summaries of the four novels.

————.,editor. *Elizabethan Prose Fiction*. New York: Odyssey Press, 1967. An anthology of important Elizabethan prose fiction which includes an essay on Deloney's place among other Elizabethan prose writers.

NEILL, S. DIANA. *A Short History of the English Novel*. London: Jarrolds Publishers, 1951. Offers a brief discussion of Deloney's novels, claiming *Jack of Newbury* is "the best of these tales."

OKAMOTO, SEIKEI. "Realism e no Sekkin—Thomas Deloney no Sakuhin ni tsuite" [Approach to Realism—On the Works of Thomas Deloney]. *Eibungaku-shi* (Hosie-diagaku), No. 4 (March 1961), 4–13. Translated by Toshibumi Kato. Reviews the novels and concludes that although Deloney contributes nothing to the concept of unity in prose fiction, his realistic characters and plots elevate him above Lyly, Sidney, and Nashe as prose writers.

PARKER, DAVID. "*Jack of Newbury*: A New Source." *English Language Notes*, 10 (1973), 172–80. Sees the ballad "A Gest of Robyn Hode" as a source for *Jack of Newbury*.

PÄTZOLD, KURT-MICHAEL. "Thomas Deloney and the English Jest-Book Tradition." *English Studies*, 53 (1972), 313–28. Discusses Deloney's close proximity to the jest books in terms of narrative details and events.

————. "Thomas Deloneys *Thomas of Reading* und das Jest Book *The Pinder of Wakefield*: Eine Vergleichende Interpretation." *Neuphilologische Mitteilungen*, 72 (1971), 113–26. Compares the structure of Deloney's novel to the jest book. A detailed analysis of the structure of both works.

POWYS, LLEWELYN. "Thomas Deloney." *Virginia Quarterly Review*, 9 (1933), 578–94. An encomium to Deloney outlining "the astonishing genius of this great Elizabethan novelist." Does not discuss the poetry.

RAMSEY, PETER. *Tudor Economic Problems*. London: Victor Collancz, Ltd., 1963. Uses new statistical data to comment upon problems of inflation, the rise of the middle class, enclosures, and the expansion of trade in Tudor England. Good discussions of the cloth industry and of the role of guilds in an expanding economy.

————, ed. *The Price Revolution in Sixteenth-Century England*. London Methuen and Company, Ltd., 1971. A collection of essays on the period of great inflation in Tudor England. Although he admits that the causes of the inflationary spiral are puzzling, he suggests simply that "productivity had failed to match population growth."

REUTER, OLE. "Some Aspects of Thomas Deloney's Prose Style." *Neuphilologische Mitteilungen*, 49 (1939), 23–72. A thorough review of Deloney's reputation, along with an analysis of his prose works.

———. "Thomas Deloney's *Thomas of Reading* and *The Pinder of Wakefield*." *Neuphilologische Mitteilungen*, 77 (1976), 599–607. Refutes the thesis by Kurt-Michael Pätzold (*supra*) that Deloney was indebted to the jest book *The Pinder of Wakefield* for some of the episodes in *Thomas of Reading*. Reuter believes that Pinder could not have been compiled before 1609, over ten years after the publication of *Thomas of Reading*, The jest book would therefore have had to use Deloney's work as a source; or, more likely, both were derived from "earlier Elizabethan sources."

ROLLINS, HYDER E. "The Black-Letter Broadside Ballad." *PMLA*, 34 (1919), 258–339. A thorough discussion of the history of street-ballad publication during the late sixteenth century. Deloney is described as one of only a few "distinguished writers" of the ballad.

———. "Thomas Deloney's Euphuistic Learning and *The Forest*." *PMLA*, 59 (1935), 679–86. Points out that Deloney got his euphuistic learning not from Latin and Italian works, but from copying passages from the English compilation *The Forest* (1571) by Thomas Fortescue.

———. "Deloney's Sources for Euphuistic Learning." *PMLA*, 51 (1936), 399–406. Identifies two works besides Thomas Fortescue's *The Forest* as sources for Deloney's descriptions of natural history and "erudite-looking anecdotes": Stephen Batman's *The Doome warning all men to the Iudegements* (1581) and Thomas Johnson's *Cornucopiae, or diuers secrets . . . Newlie drawen out of diuers Latine Authors into English* (1595).

SCHLAUCH, MARGARET. *Antecedents of the English Novel, 1400–1600: from Chaucer to Deloney*. London: Oxford University Press, 1963. Discusses Deloney's contributions of practical experience with realistic subjects to the jest book tradition in English literature.

SIEVERS, RICHARD. "Thomas Deloney: Eine Studie über Balladenlitteratur der Shakespere Zeit. Nebst Neudruck von Deloney's Roman *Jack of Newbury*." *Palaestra*, 36 (1904), 1–146. A sketch of Deloney's life and brief summaries of his novels precede a classification and discussion of the ballads. Presents the known sources and brief summaries of the ballads.

STONE, LAWRENCE. *Crisis of the Aristocracy, 1558–1641*. Oxford: The Clarendon Press, 1965. A thorough review of the breakdown of the monarchical, aristocratic government and its reformation after being modified along commonwealth interests. Statistical charts show changing means of production and changing distributions of national income. Stone fleshes out his statistical framework with discussions of changes in the nature of politics, in ethical values, and in attitudes of citizens to the monarchy, rank, privilege, business, marriage, and the commonwealth. This work is of primary importance as a collection of facts concerning, and a commentary on, social and economic forces at work in England from 1558 to 1641.

——. *The Causes of the English Revolution, 1529–1642*. London: Routledge and Kegan Paul, 1972. Reviews the history and discusses the complex causes of the breakdown of hierarchal order in sixteenth- and seventeenth-century England. What survived from the revolution after a kind of hierarchy returned in 1660 was a general concept of rule based on "the consent of a broad spectrum of society." This book brings up to date his *Crisis of the Aristocracy* (*supra*).

THIRSK, JOAN. *Economic Policy and Projects: The Development of a Consumer Society in Early Modern England*. Oxford: The Clarendon Press, 1978. Shows how the English desire for foreign goods caused a "deliberate government policy to foster the native manufacture of consumer goods." The expanded domestic manufacture of consumer goods helped to change the nature of English economic history.

WAGENKNECHT, EDWARD. *Cavalcade of the English Novel*. New York: Henry Holt and Company, 1954. Discusses Deloney as "an Elizabethan Dickens."

WRIGHT, LOUIS B. *Middle-Class Culture in Elizabethan England*. Chapel Hill: The University of North Carolina Press, 1935. A thorough scholarly study of everyday life in Elizabethan England. Discusses the great amount of literature written for and by commonplace Englishmen "without a knowledge of which a complete understanding of the age is impossible."

Index